A South Bronx 'Memoirito' of boyhood and Catholic school

DAVID PÉREZ

Illustrations by George Pérez

Wow!
Copyright © 2011 by David Pérez

All rights reserved. No part of this book
may be reproduced or transmitted in any form or by any means
without written permission from the publisher.

ISBN 978-0-983174-70-7

Cover and Interior Illustrations by George Pérez

Cover and Interior Design and Layout
by Desktop Miracles. Stowe, VT

Printed in the United States of America

The author would like to acknowledge the following:

The chapter "A Fine Boy!" appeared in the July 2010 online issue of *The Acentos Review* under the title "Tough as Bulls."

An early version of "First Date" was published in the May 2010 issue of the online journal *Imitation Fruit* under the title "First Kiss."

Excerpts from "Getting Saved" were included in the 2010 issue of *Chokecherries*, the annual anthology of the Society of the Muse of the Southwest (SOMOS).

Audio recordings of readings from "First Date" and "Christmas Cribs" are available at the website of Cultural Energy, a media organization in Taos, NM. Visit www.culturalenergy.org.

For Veronica, who is love

❖ ❖ ❖

*With love to family: Belinda, Jase, Jelayne, and my parents,
Jorge Pérez and Luz María Izquierdo*

Contents

ONE	"A Fine Boy!"	9
TWO	Flying Chalk	19
THREE	Off the Curb	25
FOUR	Getting Saved	31
FIVE	"Baseball and Ballantine"	44
SIX	"Desperadoes in Black Robes"	49
SEVEN	"*Lenguas Sabrosas*"	58
EIGHT	Christmas Cribs	63
NINE	First Date	79
TEN	Cons to the Rescue	94
ELEVEN	"Brother, I Can't Get Hit"	99
TWELVE	The Greatest Race Ever	111
THIRTEEN	"Way to Go!"	117

ONE

"A Fine Boy!"

Nineteen sixty-four. Springtime at Public School 65, 141st Street and Cypress Avenue, in the Mott Haven section of the South Bronx—before the South Bronx became the "South Bronx," when the ghetto-in-progress still smelled of paint, cheap asphalt and jobs.

Mami picked me up at the school's front entrance. Across the street stood rows of red and gray brick tenement buildings, laundry hanging on clotheslines strung along the fire escapes. From the windows, the smell of fried food filled the air, like incense.

"How was school today, *mijo*?"

"Fine, Mami."

"*Pareces triste.*"

"No, I'm okay."

Actually I was a little sad. The night before, Mami had said she was thinking of transferring my brother, George, and me to St. Luke's, the neighborhood parochial school shaped like a cinder block and attached to St. Luke's Church.

"You boys need a better school, yes?" Mami had said.

George was gung ho. "Yea! I don't like PS 65 anymore, Mami. It's getting too rough; too many fights."

I felt less enthused. I'd made friends at the school and gotten high grades. In my last report card, I'd scored an Excellent in almost every subject and was "learning to speak in complete sentences." But George was right about the rough part. That morning in the schoolyard, a girl had punched another girl in the face, calling her a "fucking motherfucker."

I was already familiar with St. Luke's, having enrolled earlier that year in catechism, the minimissionary class where I took my first steps into Roman Catholic citizenry. There, Sister Anne—a pretty nun with hazel eyes and spotless alabaster skin—taught with vigor and enthusiasm, peppering her questions in rapid succession as if we were on a television game show:

"How many apostles did Jesus have?"

"Twelve!" our class chimed.

"And what is the Holy Trinity?"

"God the Father, God the Son and God the Holy Spirit!"

It was rote learning for the most part, but endlessly infuriating. Whenever I didn't quite understand the material, it was explained away.

Sister Anne: "God has no beginning and God has no end. He is eternal and…yes, David?"

Me (incredulously): "You mean he just popped out of nowhere?"

Sister Anne: "No, God always was."

Me: "Always?"

Sister Anne: "Always."

Me: "But…"

Sister Anne (euphorically): "Such is the wonder of God! We have to accept that He is a mystery."

George had also taken catechism class, but believed all answers to Roman Catholic mysteries could be found in Thor comic books. Aasgard, he insisted, was in another dimension, "like Heaven." Odin had a white beard, so he was "God."

◆ ◆ ◆

Mami and I walked the four blocks to our apartment at 600 East 137th Street, which was part of the Millbrook Houses, a twelve-acre complex that ran from 135th to 137th streets, from Cypress Avenue to the east to Brook Avenue to the west. In 1958, when we moved there, the projects sparkled with newness: a virtual minicity with nine sixteen-story high-rises surrounded by crisp lawns, newly planted trees, spacious parking lots, a community center and six playgrounds that George and I explored in matching red tricycles.

The projects were also fireproof, which would come in handy in later years, when the South Bronx ignited into the national consciousness as the arson capital of the United States.

But before we got home, I made my daily pit stop at Joe's, my favorite watering hole for sweets and egg creams. Mami gave me ten cents and said she'd wait outside.

"Not too much candy, *mijo*."

Joe was a Mr. Potato Head-looking Arab man with thick eyebrows and hairballs the size of Milk Duds in his ears. He kept eye contact with me when I reached behind the counter to get my usual dosage of Tootsie Rolls and Now and Laters.

"You want cavities?"

"Sure," I said, smiling at Joe with my crooked teeth. Actually, I'd already paid dearly for my sweet tooth, courtesy of the Guggenheim Dental Clinic, an alleged health facility synonymous with savagery: cavity filling through trauma. I was a nine-year-old with two fillings and counting.

"Stay good in school," Joe said, as I forked over my dime. "Nothing more important."

Worries about school and teeth aside, today was a special day. When Mami and I walked through our front door, Pops was unpacking an RCA combination console that included a nineteen-inch color television, a phonograph and an AM/FM radio. This was our first major league electronics purchase since my parents moved to the Bronx from Puerto Rico.

"I love credit," Pops crowed.

Buying on credit was new for the Pérez family, a result of my father's steady work history, beginning as a migrant worker at the age of twelve, picking spinach in rural Pennsylvania.

According to Pops, he had arrived at the farm with his older brother Ricardo and two other friends. The owner met them at the gate and said to Ricardo, "How many are with you?"

"Four."

"I see only three."

Ricardo pointed at Pops. "And this guy."

"He's only a kid."

"He works harder than you."

Pops was hired. He made a dollar fifty a day.

After that, Pops toiled at various jobs, from painting houses and simonizing cars to sweeping fish guts off the sidewalks of the Fulton Street Fish Market in downtown New York.

Keeping with the food theme, Pops was now working in the meatpacking industry as a "pumper," draining blood from the carcasses of cattle and reinjecting them with water. The job paid union wages; this allowed Mami to be a full-time housewife, which she wanted, especially after her first job at a garment factory in Astor Place, cutting trimmings from bathing suits.

"As exciting as eating dirt," Mami had told us.

To celebrate the wonder of credit, my parents went shopping in El Barrio—Spanish Harlem. They purchased the requisite

Puerto Rican furniture: a bedroom set made of pressed wood, sofas and chairs with the ubiquitous plastic covering, mattresses on spring metal frames, porcelain figurines ranging from sad-eyed kittens to swirling Spanish maidens and a painting of *The Last Supper.*

Now the RCA console. When Pops took it out of the huge box he stroked it lovingly, the same way he did the prime slabs of beef he brought home from work. George, who'd missed school today with a slight cold, came out of the bedroom we shared and saw our new family member.

"Oh boy, it's a monster!"

George was a year older than me and looked more like Pops, with dark brown eyes and a glower. Unlike me, George was a planned child, a product of grand design, which earned him the affectionate nickname of Papo, a sort of "male heir" title.

My moniker, thankfully spoken only at home, was Chiquitín, which roughly translates into "really little boy."

George and I bounced up and down as Pops placed the console center stage in the living room in front of the sofa and vinyl recliner, a.k.a. the Daddy Chair. Mami fiddled with the radio knobs as I looked down into the record player.

"You could fit a half-dozen 45s in there!" I said.

"We don't have any 45s," George countered.

"Now we can get some. We have money, right Pops?"

He shooed me away, connected the antenna and turned on the TV. There in hazy shades of green and pink were Ralph and Alice Kramden having an argument. We all sat down while Pops adjusted the antenna ears and experimented with the horizontal controls.

"*Dejalo quieto,* Jorge," my mother complained as my father kept fiddling with the color even when the reception was fine. Itch scratched, he grabbed a Ballantine beer, his third of the young evening, and announced, "It's an RCA."

Then we watched *The Honeymooners.*

During a commercial break, Mami reiterated her desire to have her sons go to Catholic school. Pops took a swallow of beer.

"I like those nuns, too," he said. "They're like my mother. Tough as bulls."

"*Ay*, Jorge, that's not the reason I want to change them to St. Luke's. It's a better school, *punto*, end of story."

"I tell you boys the story about my mother? What she did when I was eight?" Pops asked George and me.

We shook our heads. Pops, like Mami, was born and raised in Tomás de Castro, a country hamlet in Caguas, Puerto Rico (they were also born the same year, 1931).

"I was eight years old, *un nene*," Pops began. "It was 1939. I come home from school—five miles I walk every day! My mother looks at me. 'Go to work.' So I went over to our bull and..."

"Wait, Pops, an *actual* bull?" I asked.

"Yeah, no big deal. *Tenemos vacas, necesitamos toros.* We have cows; we need bulls. It's a farm!" Pops polished off his beer and continued, "So I say to myself, 'Take a ride on the bull.' I get on like a *vaquero* and start laughing. My mother catches me and *bing!* hits me with a leather whip. Here, look."

Pops rolled up his left pants leg and pointed to a scar on his calf.

"Cool," I said.

He rolled down his pants leg and smiled. Mami sighed.

"*Ay*, I hear that story so many times. *Mira*, Jorge, the nuns are not crazy like your mother. St. Luke's is a good school, okay?"

Pops shrugged. "Okay, Lucy, you decide what to do and you tell me."

He pointed to the television. Ralph Kramden was threatening to send Alice "to the moon."

"You see, he's like the nuns," Pops said. "Pow! Zoom!"

"A Fine Boy!"

❖ ❖ ❖

On the last day of public school, my mother informed my third grade teacher, Mrs. Daum, of her decision to transfer me to Catholic school. When Mami and I walked into the classroom that afternoon, she noticed an attendance sheet Scotch-taped to the wall next to the front door. Posted next to our names were a series of that grand, exalted symbol of elementary school achievement: the gold star.

"Look, *mijo*, you got a lot of stars," she said.

"I got the most, Mami."

"Now you do the same in St. Luke's, yes?"

"I guess."

Mrs. Daum rose from behind her desk to greet us. She was statuesque, with a smile as wide as a canoe. She asked us to please sit, and Mami gave her the news.

"David should do well in St. Luke's," Mrs. Daum said. "The teachers here at PS 65 are good, but a lot of kids just can't keep up. It's a language problem."

The "problem" she meant was that many of my Puerto Rican classmates' first language was Spanish. Like me, they came from families that had migrated to the United States in the early 1950s, spurred on by Operation Bootstrap, a massive U.S. government–sponsored industrialization campaign that disrupted the agrarian lives of thousands of families on the island.

A large number of these families settled in the Bronx, and my generation would become the first Puerto Ricans to be born and raised in New York City.

Wanting to make it in the United States, Mami and Pops were determined to have their kids learn English. I spoke my first English word when I was two. Tugging on my mother's polka dot apron, I said, "*Mira*, Mami, *puedo hablar inglés*."

After a dramatic pause, I said, "Wow."

With my parents' encouragement, I had mastered English mainly through reading Marvel and DC comic books out loud with George. Later, watching hours of TV helped too.

Mrs. Daum beamed at me. "Yes, David is a fine boy!" she exclaimed. I beamed back. Those were the exact words my teacher had written in my final report card: "David is a fine boy!"

"You're making a good decision," Mrs. Daum told my mother as we got up to leave. "Times are changing, but good luck to David."

"*Gracias*," Mami said.

Times were changing indeed. In less than a decade, PS 65 would become the lowest-ranking elementary school in New York City. Heroin would seep into my Mott Haven neighborhood like an oil spill, and the South Bronx would become a place where danger lurked at every corner.

But first there was Catholic school to survive. And it would turn out that Pops was right: Nuns were "tough as bulls."

TWO

Flying Chalk

Fourth grade began innocently enough. My teacher, Miss McDowell, a middle-aged woman with hair as red as Lucille Ball's, was one of a handful of lay teachers at St. Luke's. Her classroom was as orderly as she was, wooden desks lined in a row like sentries, unmarked and polished to a sunny glow.

Miss McDowell taught in a direct meat-and-potatoes manner: math lesson followed by a homework assignment, spelling followed by more homework, and so on. She didn't teach religion, however. That honor fell to Sister Judith.

In the third week of school, while Sister Judith wrote a lesson on the chalkboard, my new friend Julio leaned over to whisper to a girl in front of him. Without warning, Sister Judith pivoted 180 degrees and fired her chalk. It hit Julio right between the eyes, in the soft spot just above his nose. Julio sat there, blinking and stunned. Sister Judith smoothed down her starched habit and adjusted her wire glasses. She resumed her teaching: "So God said to Moses…"

I didn't know whether to stare at poor Julio or continue scribbling in my composition notebook. Somebody whispered, "Oh man." Muffled chuckles followed. Sister Judith turned around and exhaled a lungful of air.

"I *said* Moses saw the *burning* bush!"

Exodus it was.

At lunch period, I sat next to Julio in the school cafeteria. The cherry welt on the bridge of his nose looked like an angry pimple.

"Boy, that was something," I said.

"That was embarrassing." Julio pouted. "To be decked by an old nun. How you gonna do that to somebody? I wasn't doin' nothin'."

"Maybe Sister Judith should pitch for the Yankees," I said, biting into a mushy grilled cheese sandwich.

"Maybe we should call her Deadeye," added Chino, another new recruit to St. Luke's from public school. My neighborhood had hordes of guys named Chino—and girls named China—whose Asiatic features were inherited from the Taino Indians, the original inhabitants of Puerto Rico.

"Deadeye. I like that," Julio said, his fork wandering aimlessly over a gloomy order of string beans.

"Too bad she tested her aim on you!" Chino roared, prompting a "hush!" from Sister Paul, the school principal who, alongside a trio of fellow nuns, roamed the lunchroom alternating admonishments to wrongdoers with praises to those who drank all their milk.

"These nuns are Dominican," I said.

Julio's pebble eyes bore into me. "No they're not. They're not even Spanish."

"Not the Dominican Republic, you dummy; the Dominican Order. That's like, you know, their fraternity."

"Their what?"

"Fraternity. It means club."

"Then why don't you just say that?" said Chino.

"I'm just trying—"

"Look," interrupted Julio, "Dominican, Puerto Rican, *judío*, who cares?"

At the table in front of us, a group of girls were giggling and pointing at Julio. One of them made brief eye contact with me and smiled before resuming her meal.

"Who's that girl?" I asked Julio, tilting my head in the girl's direction.

"That's Linda Ramos. She lives in the projects."

"Millbrook? That's where I live too."

"Good, you can climb up her freaking window."

Linda Ramos had luxurious eyebrows, as thick and black as a tarantula's leg. She reminded me of Annette Funicello, my current heartthrob from the Mickey Mouse Club.

"Say, David, you better stop staring before Deadeye throws something at you," Chino said.

"She's pretty."

"You're stupid," Chino replied as he and Julio got up and left.

I rose to put away my food tray and stole another peek at Linda Ramos. She eyed me back and giggled. I wiggled my fingers in that classic hello motion. She giggled again. I bumped into Sister Judith.

"Are you finished, young man?"

"Uh, yes, Sister Judith. That was a good grilled cheese sandwich."

"Out."

Recess at St. Luke's was the same as at PS 65, a period of organized mayhem with kids playing assorted games and screaming as if they'd just been released from a penitentiary.

Undoubtedly inspired by Deadeye's flying chalk, my pals were engaged in a rather uncivil game of dodgeball. Chino had just nailed a cowering Julio in the back of the head. Julio picked up the maroon ball and fired it back at Chino.

"Hey, you're supposed to be out of the game," Chino said, ducking away from the throw.

"Not in this schoolyard," Julio replied.

It was true. In St. Luke's' version of dodgeball, players walked in and out of the game at will. When I first played, my side had fifteen players. Within minutes we were down to five and then back up to ten.

It was years before I realized dodgeball had rules, including that using inferior teammates as human shields is considered valid dodgeball practice. Also, according to the National Amateur Dodgeball Association, the winning team is the one with the last person left on the court. This never happened at St. Luke's. There were, in fact, no teams to speak of, only a horde of screaming kids with fire in their eyes, aiming for someone else's head—or groin.

Opting out of recess bedlam, I strolled up to my brother, George, who was sitting on the iron railing surrounding the schoolyard. As per our new custom, we traded information about the day's happenings: I told him about Sister Judith's marksmanship while he spilled the beans on his fifth grade teacher, Sister Marcellina, a feisty servant of God pushing seventy.

"Today she smacked this girl Brenda on the palm with her ruler," George said.

"Did she cry?"

"Nope, she didn't even flinch."

"Tough chicks here," I said, remembering the girl bully at PS 65. "But tougher nuns. Miss McDowell is nice, though. They should let her teach religion too."

"You gotta be a nun. You know, training and stuff."

As we spoke, Sister Paul came out of the cafeteria and clanged her brass bell, which signaled that recess was over and it was time to line up and return to class.

Julio appeared not to have heard the call to order and continued running around with the dodgeball. Sister Paul approached him and clunked him on the head with the bell.

"Ouch," Julio cried.

The guy's not having a good day, I thought.

To be fair, though, not every nun in St. Luke's was scary nor were they always on edge, ready to pounce on some hapless soul. As fourth grade chugged along, my religion teacher, Sister Judith, was downright gentle most of the time, smiling at us when she unveiled mystery after mystery of the Catholic faith, like God creating the world in six days and resting on the seventh, an act of laziness I thought unworthy of the Almighty. Why did He need to rest?

Miss McDowell was always kind in her demeanor. She patted our heads whenever we answered a question correctly, especially with spelling. She was also extremely patient with some of the slower students, particularly Renaldo, a Stan Laurel look-alike who muttered, "I don't understand it" every time he was called on to read something aloud. Miss McDowell would lean over his desk and say in a delicate voice, "Okay, Renaldo, let's read it together: 'The very big store was very far away…'"

"I don't understand it."

"Say it slowly, Renaldo. 'The very big store.'"

"The, uh, very big…"

"Store."

"Store…"

"…was very far away."

"I don't understand it!"

I wanted to scream.

Miss McDowell encouraged us to order books from the Scholastic Book Club for Kids newsletter. My favorite was *Strange Tales*. The ad screamed, "A collection of bizarre stories, all of them true!"

When the book arrived, I devoured the rip-roaring accounts of ghosts, sea monsters and aliens from other planets. Each chapter challenged its readers to "believe it or not!"

One tale has stayed with me all these years.

A night watchman in Australia is guarding a warehouse. In that warehouse are coffins to be put on a ship. Many coffins. All of a sudden, the ground shakes. It's a great shake, like an earthquake. The watchman goes inside the warehouse. He finds the coffins open, with all the bodies gone!

When I shared the story with George, he said, "That's like when the disciples found out Jesus was resurrected from the dead!"

"I guess Catholics aren't the only ones with mysteries."

THREE

Off the Curb

In my neighborhood, tests of manhood started early. According to Chino, he'd already been in five fights before coming to St. Luke's—and he was ready to kick ass again. He had also "felt up a whole bunch of *mamis*."

"Chicks are easy," he informed me.

Chino didn't believe in hitting girls, though. In fact, you were a punk if you even got in a fight with them. "Except when they really mess with you."

Meanwhile I had my own toughening up to do. I wasn't getting it through dodgeball. For one thing, I stunk at it. My throws were anemic, my aim atrocious. At one point my throw rudely interrupted a game of Double Dutch.

Julio came to the rescue by introducing Find the Belt. The rules were simple: one player hid a belt. The other players, about five in total, looked for it, with the player who hid it letting them know if they were warm or cold. When someone found the belt, he or she went after the others, swinging the belt at their fleeing flesh.

"I definitely want to play!" I told Julio.

But when Sister Paul discovered what the game was about—Julio had emerged from underneath a nearby-parked car and yelled, "Run!" with a leather belt held high over his head—she insisted there "would be none of that in St. Luke's!"

And then Sister Paul clunked Julio on the head again.

At Millbrook, stating that it was my invention, I introduced Find the Belt to some of my new friends there. Sunshine, my next-door neighbor whose nickname came from his yellow teeth, thought it a fabulous idea.

"Whoever gets hit the most should be champion!" he said.

"But the point is not to get hit."

"That's not as fun."

Find the Belt was a smash success. I got in a few licks, received a couple of welts, everyone was happy. Then Sunshine brought in a garrison belt to raise the stakes.

"Those belts are too thick," I said. "Plus you might hit someone with them big buckles."

"That's why it's cool, man."

No one else thought it cool, so the game was history.

I was left with sports, but I stunk at them too. The summer before school began, I had played in the Mushball League, organized by the Millbrook Community Center. Although Mushball was played with a soft version of a softball, the bats were solid wood. It didn't matter. I was dreadful. I rode the bench for virtually the entire ten-game season.

In time, I sought my redemption with Off the Curb, a popular after-school game played in the Little Park, the playground in front of my project building, 600 East 137th Street.

The aim of the game was to throw a Spaldeen at the Curb, a meaty chunk of concrete located under the fence near the park's front entrance. If you angled your throw right, the pink ball would bounce off the Curb and go sailing over the fence on the opposite side of the Little Park—a whopping twenty-five yards.

The rules of Off the Curb were similar to baseball, except there was no pitcher or catcher, and you only got one throw of the ball. First base was next to the concrete turtle, which was missing half its head. Second base was a square box chalked into the ground about twenty feet from the turtle's hind legs. Third base was one of the concrete barrels, and home base was the Curb.

Collis, a twelve-year-old Black kid, practically an elder, was the official Off the Curb home run king. According to a shadowy yet universally accepted honor system, Collis had amassed fifty-eight home runs. He used a sidearm throw like a whip. I tried to imitate his technique, but the Spaldeen kept ricocheting into my chest and, one time, into my face, knocking me flat on my ass.

One day after school, I finished homework early and went downstairs to practice my throw with my pal Lefty. I too threw left-handed, even though I wrote with my right hand.

Lefty didn't share my dilemma. He approached the curb from a rigid standing position, throwing the ball downward at a forty-five-degree angle. It didn't look cool at all, but it worked. Lefty already had thirty home runs.

"Just throw it like I do, " Lefty said.

"But you look so stiff."

"Yeah, but I can hit home runs, Dave. You can't."

"I like the way Collis whips the ball, but I guess I should try it your way."

"Hey, don't do it for me, man. You wanna keep kissing the ball with your face, that's your problem."

As we discussed the uniqueness of our left arms, more guys streamed into the Little Park. A game of Off the Curb was announced. Collis and Lefty appointed themselves captains and chose sides.

"I pick Fat Ray, " Collis said.

"I got Sunshine."

"I got Chumpy."

"Yo, my name's Armando!"

"Shut up, Chumpy."

Lefty looked around. "I'll take David."

"You can have him," Collis said.

Eventually five guys were picked for each team. The game began.

My side batted first, and Sunshine led off with a single. Then it was my turn.

I looked at Lefty, nodded, and threw the ball like he did. Bingo! The ball sailed over the fence: a shot heard around the world. Everyone hooted and clapped as I circled the bases. Reaching home base, I shrugged like it was no big thing.

"About time," Collis said.

My team got slaughtered, 24 to 6. But I did get another hit, a double.

FOUR

Getting Saved

Back at St. Luke's, I kept getting top grades in all my subjects. Replacing the two public school categories of "Social Behavior" and "Personal Hygiene" were two distinct Catholic school brands: "Obeys Promptly" and "Is Reverent in Religious Duties."

Reverence entailed, among other things, being properly solemn when reciting the Our Father or Hail Mary and showing up for Mass every Sunday. It also involved climbing the sacrament ladder.

Sacraments were vital to becoming a good Catholic, and like all sacred ceremonies, one had to receive them in the proper order. Sacrament number one was Baptism, which had purified my two-month soul of original sin by sprinkling my head with holy water.

Mami says I cried throughout the Baptismal affair. When I point out I was a baby, she says that the problem was that I was a sickly infant who was "born crying and never stopped—ever." I had rashes all over my fair-skinned body, which prompted Mami to put Ban-Lon socks on my tiny hands, lest I cut myself scratching.

"It's probably allergies," the doctors told her.

"From what?"

"We don't know."

So relentless was my crying, Mami says, that one night the building superintendent, a stout German named Boris, knocked on our door and told my mother, "You make baby no cry or I call cops." Mami, shaken and a little pissed, said she would try. *Maybe if you fixed the boiler he'd do better,* she wanted to say but didn't.

When I turned three, my allergies disappeared almost overnight. Mami says it was a miracle. Hey, why not?

So here I was, in the Year of Our Lord 1964, healthy and cleansed of original sin, but not technically "saved," i.e., qualified to enter the gates of heaven. For that honor, Sister Judith emphasized, one needed to receive sacrament *numero dos*—Holy Eucharist, commonly called Holy Communion, the transformation of bread into the Body of Jesus Christ.

But as with many things Roman Catholic, there was a catch. In order to receive Communion, one needed to be totally without sin. And to achieve that blessed state, one must have performed Confession.

I needed clarity. "Sister Judith, is Confession then another sacrament?"

"Yes, David, it is."

"So we're really doing *two* sacraments."

"That is correct, although Holy Communion is the goal. It is salvation."

Sister Judith prepared us for salvation by reviewing the two categories of sins: mortal and venial. Mortal sins were high crimes against God's law, such as murder and adultery. If you violated any of the Ten Commandments, you were in mortal sin territory and in danger of suffering "eternal damnation in hell." Venial sins were akin to misdemeanors; they didn't involve "a grave matter." They could even be accidental, as in, "Oops, I cursed." Venial sins did not result in a separation from God. They couldn't be cumulative. Ten venial sins did not become one mortal sin.

Yet, in my mind, a blurry line existed between the two types. Take stealing, for example.

"Does it matter if it's from an apartment or gas station?" Julio asked, trying hard to sound innocent.

Sister Judith sighed. "There is no difference."

"What if it's bubble gum?"

"Julio, stop it."

I raised my hand. "Yes, David?"

"What if you give the stuff back?"

Sister Judith looked up to the ceiling as if seeking divine guidance. She nodded her head and said, "Stealing is a mortal sin because it involves grievous intention. Bubble gum, dear Julio, is not a grievous matter. If you give it back, David, then it is no longer stealing, is it? Still, you should confess your sin to the Lord. But do not trouble yourselves, children. As long as you go to Confession, our Savior will forgive you."

I was still unclear.

Plus there was *another* catch. You had to be sorry for your sins. And not just sorry, but *truly* sorry. And, added the sly Sister Judith, Jesus Christ would *know* if you weren't, just as Santa Claus knew if you were naughty or nice.

Since I had no plans (yet) to become a thief or to try to hide from the all-knowing God, I took solace in Sister Judith's promise that God was just, that only wicked people doing wicked deeds ended up in the fiery pits of hell.

But just in case I tried to pull one over on the Almighty, there was the netherworld: purgatory, a limbo reserved for "moderate" sinners who needed a little suffering before being allowed into paradise, a sort of hell lite. I had a hard time envisioning where purgatory was and what it looked like. The best I could imagine was a claustrophobic dark space the size of a closet.

One afternoon Sister Paul came to our classroom. "I am going to demonstrate how to take the Eucharist," our principal said, referring to the thin oval wafer that, with the proper incantation, magically turned into the Body of Christ.

"Let it dissolve in your mouth," she said, moving her lips rapidly up and down. Sister Paul then made a distinct swallowing sound.

"Thank you, Sister Paul," said Sister Judith, clapping her hands in appreciation.

I thought it rather odd to be shown Communion culinary practices. On the other hand, this was the Son of God we were talking about. Letting "His Body" melt in your mouth correctly was probably important.

Julio said it was "like eating M&Ms."

❖ ❖ ❖

Saturdays were the official Confession day. In their infinite wisdom, the Church fathers considered it best for people to have twenty-four hours or less to be without sin. Ideally you confessed, went home, stayed pure (in thought and deed), and slept (*on Saturday night!*). The next morning, you retained your purity through Sunday Mass and received your Communion. Then you repeated the entire process the following week, and the week after that, ad infinitum. That is, if you continued to have weekly sins, and who wouldn't?

On the Saturday before my first Holy Communion, I was nervous. There is an art to Confession. Besides the not-so-simple tasks of remembering your sins and being truly repentant, you must pick the right priest to confess to. My brother, George, urged me to check out Father Dalton, the resident hippie cleric and the only priest to have actually graduated from St. Luke's.

"He likes to crack jokes," George explained. "Plus, he's light with penance. But the line to see him can be really long. Father Kelly's okay, I guess, but he gives a *lot* of prayers."

"What about Father Miguel?"

"I've never gone to him. He has a thick accent, so you need to pay attention."

"He's a Spanish Franciscan priest," I said.

"Well, there you go."

I opted for Father Dalton, got in line and began reviewing my list of trespasses and transgressions. As expected, it had proven extremely difficult to recall all my sins. How can any person remember each time he or she lied, each time he or she said or *thought* "shit" and "fuck"? I found myself balancing between actually remembering and simply inventing numbers because they sounded right.

In the end, I settled on five lies, five curses and thrice taking the name of the Lord God in vain. These seemed reasonable amounts.

When my turn arrived, I pushed aside the red velvet curtain and entered the dark booth. I knelt down. A wood window panel slid open to reveal the shadowy figure of Father Dalton, his face obscured by a wire-mesh screen. The ritual began.

"Bless me, Father, for I have sinned," I said, crossing myself. "This is my first Confession."

"Welcome aboard."

I recited my litany of lies, curses and the misuse of God's hallowed name.

"This is your first Confession, and that's all you have?"

I began to fidget. What else should I say?

"Uh, well, I peeked at this girl's panties once, Father."

"What kind of sin is that?"

"Coveting?"

Father Dalton laughed and asked if I were truly sorry. I told him I was.

"Okay, my son, recite two Our Fathers and one Hail Mary." He garbled something in Latin and slid the panel closed. I felt relieved. Just three prayers? Head bowed, I found a pew and knelt on the padded kneeling cushion. Feeling fresh and forgiven, I said my prayers in a measured, hushed tone.

The next day was our first Holy Communion. I wore the regulatory first Communion outfit: dark blue polyester suit, starched white shirt, white satin clip-on tie, folded white handkerchief in breast pocket, and white bow and band worn over the left jacket sleeve. The girls wore frilly white dresses with white veils and white gloves: little Christian brides.

We paraded into St. Luke's in two lines: boys on the right side, girls on the left. Polaroid cameras clicked and whirred as legions of proud parents and relatives sought out their newly minted angels.

The First Communion Class of '65 sat in the first four pews. Mami was in pew five, resplendent in an orange print dress and fake pearl necklace. Her dark hair was flipped at the ends, framing a smile of perfect teeth. George sat next to her, looking bored in a tan suit jacket and plaid bow tie.

Pops wasn't there, opting to sleep late after a night of drink and dominoes with his buddies from the meatpacking factory. As it turned out, Pops never attended any of my church or school events. He said Mami and God were there, so why should *he* bother?

Monsignor Mulcahey, the pastor of St. Luke's, led Mass; Father Kelly and Father Dalton assisted. Pushing eighty, Monsignor Mulcahey had been the pastor at St. Luke's forever. A Bing Crosby look-alike, he wore an ankle-length black robe with red trimming and big buttons.

It was a long Mass containing an even longer sermon. I looked around the church, counting cracks on the mustard-colored marble pillars, round as cannons. Stained-glass windows depicted scenes from the Gospel of St. Luke: parables about the good Samaritan, the prodigal son and the barren fig tree. Beneath the windows were hand-carved reenactments of the Stations of the Cross with Jesus's name spelled with a *v* instead of a *u*, an Old English thing.

 The *Phantom of the Opera* organ music soared as the moment neared for us to receive the sacred wafer.

 "Take this bread and eat from it, for this is my Body," Monsignor Mulcahey intoned, raising the wafer aloft with two bony hands. With a similar invocation, he turned the wine, kept in a solid gold chalice, into the Blood of Christ. But only he dranketh from that cup.

 I began my slow walk to the altar. Julio was in front of me, the back of his neck shiny with sweat. I stayed focused, my hands in prayer position, Johnson's Baby Powder keeping my neck dry.

 Finally I was at the railing. To my left, rows of candles flickered in crimson glasses. A life-sized crucifix towered over the marble altar; Jesus's brown eyes stared off into the distance, waiting for death. Monsignor Mulcahey took a wafer from a second chalice.

 "The Body of Christ," he said.

 "Amen," I said. I closed my eyes and stuck out my tongue.

 I expected to feel instantly holy, to hear trumpets. Instead, I could only think of how remarkably plain the wafer tasted. One would think the church would at least season the bread to match its stated wondrous purpose. I dissolved the bread in my mouth using the Sister Paul method and soaked in the lifted voices of the four-member St. Luke's choir.

 Afterward, our first Communion class accepted hugs and congratulations as if we'd just won the World Series. George patted my back, and Mami pinched my cheek.

 I walked over to Julio. "Hey man," I said, slapping him five.

"That was rough," he said, his bubble lips breaking into a grin. "And we got to do this every week!"

"At least it won't be the first anymore."

My mother called me over and told me we had to go to the next, equally vital part of Holy Communion: the official photo shoot. We headed down 138th Street to Victor's Studio, a block away from St. Luke's Church and right next door to the sadly popular John's Bargain Store, a discount shop of cardboard bins overflowing with cheap plastic goods and Lightning sneakers that cost a dollar. "Welfare shit," we called it.

Victor's ran a brisk business, his storefront window sprinkled with framed pictures of blissful married couples and peaceful baptized infants. Several photos appeared as if the color were added as an afterthought, a pastel shading that made the primarily Puerto Rican and Black faces gleam like wax.

We stepped inside a curtained-off room equipped with a small velvet-covered pew, a hymnal with a rosary for a bookmark, and silhouetted pictures of Jesus Christ, Mary and some disciples on the back wall.

George nudged me. "The Dracula room," he whispered.

Victor, a rotund man wearing matted hair and smelling of a generous helping of Old Spice cologne, instructed me to kneel on the pew.

"Don't smile," he said. "Just think how you've received the glory of God."

"Okay."

Victor got behind his tripod-mounted camera, throwing the attached dark blanket over himself with a flourish.

"Think holy," he said.

Flash! It wasn't a bad shot, and to this day the picture remains my mother's favorite, hung on her living room wall in its ornate wheat-colored frame, my expression one of unbounded piety.

❖ ❖ ❖

Now that I was technically "saved,"—notwithstanding having to be resaved every week via Confession—one would think my journey into Roman Catholic salvation would be complete.

One would be wrong.

There remained the final sacrament of initiation: Confirmation, which, as church canon states, confirms that you are a good Christian by "bestowing upon you the seven gifts of the Holy Spirit: wisdom, understanding, knowledge, fortitude, guidance, piety and fear of the Lord."

To receive these gifts, you wore a red robe and white cotton gloves, and an actual bishop performed the rite, chanting in Latin and anointing you with the oil of chrism, a balsamic lotion from ancient times.

Guiding me through the preparation ritual was my fifth grade teacher, Sister Marcellina. She explained that since God is the Holy Trinity—God the Father, God the Son and God the Holy Spirit—Confirmation is the time "when the Holy Spirit enters our lives and makes us complete Christians."

Julio asked Sister Marcellina why the Holy Spirit was a dove. She answered that it was merely "drawn that way to convey peace and wisdom."

"So you can draw it another way?" he asked.

"Why would you want to *do* that, Julio?"

"I don't know."

"I didn't think so."

A key component of the sacrament involved choosing a Confirmation name based on your favorite patron saint or angel, someone you felt would, or should, guide and protect you. Your Confirmation name could also become your official middle name, Sister Marcellina said.

Catholics are no slouches when it comes to saints. In what seems like an attempt to cover all possibilities, there are thousands of saints for virtually everyone and everything, including saints for birds (Martin of Tours for geese) and entire countries (Our Lady of Divine Providence for Puerto Rico). Occupations assigned to saints range from beekeeping (St. Ambrose) to pallbearing (Joseph of Arimathea). Agatha is the saint of volcanic eruptions, Jude the saint of lost causes.

I picked Michael as my new middle name because he was one of only three archangels, making him powerful. That's what I wanted to be—powerful.

Mami liked my new name: David Michael Pérez. She said it sounded important.

"I picked Ann when I did my Confirmation," she said. "But I don't keep it because I already have middle name."

Mami was born Luz María Izquierdo, and her eight siblings were all raised Roman Catholic in Puerto Rico, saying grace before every meal and prayers every night before going to sleep, which Mami still did, clutching at her rosaries in front of a small statue of the Virgin Mary. Mami was devout, but never fanatical or overly stern. Hers was a steady belief, loving yet firm, and, despite my continuing befuddlement at the eternal mysteries of the Catholic faith, I found Mami's prayers asking God to "watch over" her sons comforting and reassuring.

After we talked, Mami pulled out a volume of the Funk & Wagnalls encyclopedia set from the built-in shelves. She'd bought the set with her saved-up S&H Green Stamps and placed them alongside her figurines, which she considered her private art collection. More than once, she had smacked my hands when I mistook them for action figures.

Mami read the encyclopedia more than I did—almost daily, in fact. She'd pick a volume at random and begin reading "just to find out things."

"Did you know Great Lakes are made of fresh water?"

"No, I didn't, Mami."

"Encyclopedia says they're biggest group in the world."

"Wow."

In Puerto Rico, Mami had left high school after her junior year. Her parents, while supportive of her education, needed her to help with the chores demanded by land and home: doing laundry for her large family, feeding the chickens and pigs and the relentless cooking. Mami was heartbroken. She had an ear for poetry and began writing her own poems as a teenager. She also enjoyed history and math, often sitting with George and me at the dining table when we did our homework there.

"But you do what you have to do and move on," Mami always said. She wrote in one of her poems, "*Porque la vida es dura / me hizo dura la vida*": "Because life is hard / life made me hard."

I can see now why our education was important to my mother. George and I were fulfilling the dream she had for herself.

My Confirmation came off smoothly. A bishop from the archdiocese anointed me with the consecrated oil of chrism and marked me with the sign of the cross, invoking the Holy Spirit so that I could share in Christ's "royal, priestly and prophetic honor."

Unlike Holy Communion, there was no official photo shoot after the ceremony, only a picture taken of me shaking George's hand on the steps leading to the church. I looked stoic.

After the handshake, I ran into Linda Ramos, who had also been confirmed.

"Hi, David," she said.

"Oh, hi, Linda."

"Wanna walk me home?"

I looked at Mami, who was grinning from ear to ear.

"Go ahead, *mijo*."

Linda introduced herself to Mami. "Nice to meet you, Mrs. Pérez."

"Nice to meet you, too." Mami looked at me again. "She's nice, David."

Linda blushed.

"Uh, well, let's walk, shall we?" I said.

Mami said she'd see me at home and left Linda and me to our stroll.

We walked down Cypress Avenue toward the projects, where Linda also lived. I felt giddy. Today was the first day I had put more than one sentence together with Linda, having barely talked to her since eyeing her in the lunchroom on the day Julio got clocked by Sister Judith's laser-guided chalk. I secretly considered Linda my future girlfriend.

"You're always getting high grades," she said. "I mean all the time, right?"

This time I blushed. Despite my pride, I rarely boasted about my school smarts. There was an unspoken yet loudly proclaimed law on the block that being smart and being cool simply didn't go together. In class, I took care not to raise my hand too often, even though I knew the answer to every question. However, my incessant 90s and 100s became common knowledge every time the teachers barked out grades as they handed back our quizzes and homework.

Chino had taken to sometimes calling me Brainiac, after the highly intelligent DC Comics supervillain with a bald green head shaped like a mushroom cloud. Chino had also made sure to add that being smart "wasn't shit."

"I'm not a mama's boy or anything like that, Linda," I said defensively.

"It's okay, David. I think it's good that you're smart."

"You're smart, too."

"No, I'm not. But you're sweet for saying that." *Sweet!*

I offered to help with homework if she wanted. She said no thanks and I immediately felt stupid.

We arrived at Linda's building. "Let's be friends, David," she said.

Did she mean friend friend or boyfriend?

"Sure," I said.

I bounced home, the first layer of ice broken. But it would be two years before I took the next step with Linda. And what a misstep it would be.

FIVE

"Baseball and Ballantine"

Confirmation had taken place in May, close to my birthday of May 28, so Pops decided to celebrate these two events at once by taking me to Yankee Stadium.

"You're ten years old," he said. "I already work by then."

Although we played the occasional game of catch and sometimes walked together to the bodega, going to the stadium was the first time Pops and I had spent a whole day together, just being father and son. George didn't care much for sports, baseball or otherwise, unless you included the World Wide Wrestling Federation and what had rapidly become our favorite part of it: women's wrestling.

I was the only member of the family who watched Yankee baseball with Pops. This was the era of Mickey Mantle and Roger Maris, of Whitey Ford and Bobby Richardson, a time when the Bronx Bombers were perennial World Series champions. Years later, my father would admit that he watched the games for another reason: he bet on them.

"I won some, I lost some. No big deal."

The No. 4 train to 161st Street was crowded with Yankee fans. Air-filled plastic bats jostled for space with assorted banners, flags and placards pasted with pictures of Yankee players. While my part of the South Bronx was decidedly Black and Puerto Rican, the subway car Pops and I were in was like the United Nations: varying shades of pink and brown faces, women and men, young and old, all ready to root for the home team.

When we arrived at the historic ballpark, the smell of hot dogs filled the humid air. The Yankees emerged from the dugout to a standing ovation, their famous pinstriped uniforms freshly bleached.

"Wow, this is great," I said.

"Baseball and Ballantine!" Pops yelled. On cue, a vendor arrived, expertly balancing a tray of filled-to-the-brim Ballantine beers. Pops ordered a brew and told the guy to come back soon.

Another vendor screamed, "Hey, get your hot dogs here!" With the money my father gave me—"So you have your *own* money like a man!"—I bought two hot dogs with mustard and a Coke that was three-quarters ice.

The frank was delicious, even though I knew it was mostly water and chemicals. Pops had described the ways hot dogs were processed at his job in the meatpacking factory.

"The worst meat is cold cuts," he had told me the week before at home. "*Puro* USDA shit. Baloney is the worst. Hot dogs are the next worst. We pump them with water and sodium nitrite, *puro mierda.*"

I polished off my second frank and gulped my Coca-Cola. Despite the horror stories about meat, my family remained die-hard carnivores. Besides, we always used Spanish names for our meat—*bistec* instead of beefsteak, *pernil* instead of pork shoulder—and for some odd reason, that made the meat sound better, at least to me.

After five and a half innings, neither the Yankees nor the Red Sox had scored a run. The crowd was getting restless.

"How do you feel tomorrow?" Pops asked.

Uh-oh, here comes one of Pops's lame jokes, I thought.

"Same as today, with your hands." Pops laughed and repeated the punch line, as if saying it twice would make the joke funnier. I forced a chuckle.

At the bottom of the sixth, Yankee second baseman Tom Tresh stepped up to the plate. In the seat in front of me, a kid about my age, outfitted in a Yankee cap and crinkly leather Rawlings baseball glove, began pounding his mitt.

"C'mon, Tresh, hit it in the trash!"

His blond father guffawed and mussed his blond son's hair. "Good one, son!" he said.

Good one? That was cornier than my Pops's joke.

Tresh hit a foul ball that whistled by. The toothy kid leaped and stretched out his glove, even though the ball landed a million rows away.

"Nice try, son!" the father said.

"Thanks, Popsdy!"

What is this, a freaking Leave It to Beaver *episode?*

My father patted my knee and continued looking at the game. I shifted in my chair, trying to think of something witty to add to the festivities, coveting my own Rawlings glove, wondering what was up with my flash of anger. Tom Tresh hit a single, and Clete Boyer followed with a triple. The Yankees were on their way to another victory.

On the subway ride home, I was confused. Did I want similar moments between Pops and me, full of hair mussing and sugary "gosh darns"? A *Father Knows Best* relationship?

I began waving my Yankee pennant to no one in particular and glanced over at my father, who was sleeping in his seat. His skin was shellacked from the sun, the veins on his muscled forearms thick as earthworms. Mami loved to tell me the story about how Pops, "handsome Mr. Jorge Pérez," had serenaded her with *décimas* when they were first dating, improvising lyrics about "*una mujer bonita con el nombre Luz María.*"

"He had tough life," Mami would add. "No love, just work." It must have been getting really tough lately. Pops was coming home increasingly late from work, and I sometimes overheard Mami complaining about his breath.

The No. 4 train pulled into the 125th Street station and I shook Pops awake. "It's our stop, Pops."

We transferred to the No. 6 train and got off on Brook Avenue. As we walked home, Pops kicked an empty beer bottle lying on the sidewalk into the street.

"Stupid people."

"At least it was a Ballantine," I said.

"Baseball and Ballantine!" he yelled to the night sky.

We neared home.

"Hey, Pops, how do you feel tonight?"

"You tell me."

"With your hands."

I leaned into his broad, rounded shoulders. He didn't muss my hair or put his arm around me.

SIX

"Desperadoes in Black Robes"

Carlos stood in front of the class, head down, shuffling his brown Playboy shoes. A sharp dresser who'd already been left back twice, Carlos was an eighth grader who had been summoned to our classroom by my teacher, Brother Steven, a Marine drill instructor clone with piano teeth and straw-blond crew cut hair. Carlos had entered the classroom as if dragging a ball and chain, his gaze fixed on the tile floor.

Brother Steven's deep breaths hissed like steam from a radiator. The silver cross hanging from his neck contrasted sharply with his flowing black cassock. Three different-sized paddles graced his desk.

Standing a few feet from Carlos was my classmate John Alvarez, nervous and twitchy, his matchstick arms tugging on a wool jacket two sizes too big.

"Tell me again what happened, John," Brother Steven said.

John hesitated and cleared his throat. After a few seconds he spoke.

"Um, Carlos stole from me yesterday, Brother. I was outside walking down Cypress Avenue when, um, he starting pushing me and asking for all my money."

"And what did you do?"

"I gave it to him. I only had two quarters."

"Is this true, Carlos?"

Carlos nodded. Brother Steven adjusted his thick gold-framed glasses and told John to go sit.

It was the second week of the sixth grade, the year 1965. From now through the eighth grade, my classes would be all-boys, taught under the stern supervision of the Brothers of the Sacred Heart, a gang of priest wannabes. The girls were continuing their education with the Sisters of the Dominican Order.

I'd have to wait until college until I sat in a classroom again with female students.

The Brothers of the Sacred Heart had a reputation for being some pretty nasty hombres. Rumor had it that their religious order was hatched during the Middle Ages, in some dark European castle lit by wall-mounted torches and reeking of monk sweat. The sisters had their convent in upstate New York, in a bucolic town called Blauvelt. But where was the brothers' headquarters? No one knew, or said.

Before school began, I tried to pump my brother George for information. He'd had Brother Steven the year before, but hardly ever spoke of him. George claimed a vow of silence that came with being "one of the older kids." When pressed he would say, "You'll just have to learn about them like my class did, Dave, through blood, sweat and hellfire. Just think of them as desperadoes in black robes."

Brother Steven rolled up his sleeves, exposing chiseled forearms with wisps of blond hair. "You like to pick on kids smaller than you?" he asked Carlos.

John gnawed on his lip like he was determined to swallow it. Carlos wiped away the beads of sweat that had multiplied on his forehead and looked down at his shoes again, as if his footwear offered relief from the tension. "Well? I'm waiting," Brother Steven said, voice rising.

I shifted in my seat. *Why doesn't Carlos say something?*

Brother Steven grabbed Carlos by the lapels of his jacket and hurled him against a wall. A collective gasp rose from our class. Carlos moaned.

With open palms, Brother Steven shoved Carlos hard, sending him sailing into the blackboard, his mohair jacket crumpled, shoes forgotten. We gasped again.

The assault had come quickly. Brother Steven inspected the arsenal on his desk: a thick wooden paddle about a foot long; a thinner, splintered version a few centuries old; and a bamboo cane. He picked up the cane and whipped it through the air, filling the room with a whooshing sound that sent shivers down my spine. Putting down the cane, he adjusted his glasses again and settled for the thick paddle. *Jesus, was that a smile?*

Carlos seemed to know the drill. He stifled a sob and bent over at the waist, hands on knees. Brother Steven whacked him in the backside so hard that Carlos literally hopped, the same way I later saw Joe Frazier hop after being hammered by a George Foreman uppercut in 1972.

"Did you *see* that, man?" Roberto whispered to me. Roberto was a new recruit to St. Luke's; another public school transplant whose parents thought their son needed his education mixed with religion and some good old assault and battery.

"Wow," I whispered back.

A second swing and Carlos's sobs flowed, a broken prisoner on the River Kwai. For a moment, I thought Brother Steven was going to hit Carlos again. Instead, he stood perfectly still, inhaling deeply and thoughtfully.

"Man oh man," I heard someone mutter.

Brother Steven put away his paddle. "Don't touch one of my kids again," he told Carlos.

Strangely, I felt a little like, *right on, no one's going to mess around with the guys from Brother Steven's class!* Yet it bothered me watching the brutality. It was, I don't know, just too *mean.*

Plus, as Roberto said later that day, "That protection shit's nice, but wait till Brother Steven breaks on one of us."

◆ ◆ ◆

I related the episode to my family as we ate dinner sitting down at our latest credit purchase: a maple-wood dining set with a plastic lace tablecloth. More plastic covered the padded seat cushions. A replica of da Vinci's *The Last Supper* hung on the wall over the table.

Pops had his own table: a folding tin tray placed in front of his caramel-colored vinyl recliner. This is where he *always* ate, as if perched on his own private throne.

Pops spat out a chicken bone. "If a teacher hit me like that, my father would go to the school and punch him in the neck."

"So if a teacher hits me, you'll come to school and hit him in the neck?"

Pops ignored my question and continued eating.

"I think Brother Steven was wrong," I said.

My mother agreed. "*Si, fue demasiado.* But the boy who stole was wrong, too."

"I told you he was mean," George said. "He should put notches on his paddle like a gunslinger. Does he still have that cane?"

"Yeah. He's like a prison guard. I wonder if he has tattoos."

"That teacher should go there," Pops said, pointing to the images of tanks and helicopters on the television screen. The six o'clock news was reporting on a place called Vietnam.

Mami banged her hand on the table. "Too much talk about killing and hitting. You both have just got to stay good. *Ahora,* finish your food."

After dinner, I wondered aloud to George if Brother Steven was simply protecting us, like Little Caesar knocking around wiseguys who muscled in on his turf.

"That's stupid," George replied. "But I don't know, this neighborhood is getting hard. That's why I like to stay home. Remember when we saw the *tecatos*?"

The summer before school began, George and I had been sitting in the Big Park—an inventive name given to the largest playground in the Millbrook Houses—when two teenaged guys raced by lugging huge boxes of Old London potato chips. The Old London factory was located about a mile away, on Bruckner Boulevard.

An old man sitting on the bench next to us had yelled at them, "I'm gonna call the cops!"

The guys had laughed, called him "a stupid *viejo*" and continued running. Nobody else in the park paid them any mind.

"Goddamn *tecatos*," the *viejo* had muttered when the robbers left. *Tecatos* meant heroin addicts, and I would hear the word a lot in the coming years.

I wasn't sure how the old-timer knew the guys were addicts. Their boldness? The way they laughed and talked back at him?

The man had started lamenting about how the neighborhood was "going to fucking hell." These addicts didn't even have the decency to steal stuff at night, he said, and he needed to move back to Puerto Rico, "*donde la vida es más tranquila.*"

"So maybe it's true," George said. "Maybe Brother Steven's just tormented and stuff, like the Incredible Hulk. Maybe he's worried about us."

I thought it over. "Maybe. Or maybe he's just crazy."

❖ ❖ ❖

It wasn't long before somebody in our class fell victim to Brother Steven's handiwork. Chino had forgotten his homework two days in a row, but insisted that this time he didn't *really* forget it.

"I just accidentally left it home," he said.

"Oh?"

Chino shrugged his shoulders and offered to go home and "find the homework." Brother Steven sighed, rolled up his sleeves and told Chino to "come get his medicine."

Chino sprang up from his chair and appeared unafraid. He had recently taken up boxing at St. Mary's Recreation Center and was morphing into a Puerto Rican Dennis the Menace, prone to pranks and wreaking havoc. Whenever Brother Steven was out of the room, he would put thumbtacks on people's chairs, which (speaking from experience) really stung. Even after the Carlos incident, Chino had bragged, "I ain't afraid of brothers of any heart," punctuating his words with an impressive bit of shadow boxing, left jabs and right hooks blurring the air.

Brother Steven selected the thinner paddle and instructed Chino to bend over. "Smile, you're on *Candid Camera*," he said and whacked Chino, who bounced and rubbed his ass like it was on fire.

We laughed instinctively and, surprisingly, so did Brother Steven, who put his weapon away as Chino winced in exaggeration, drawing more laughs from an appreciative audience.

It was a disarming turn of events. *Was Brother Steven tricking us?* I wondered. *Making us think that he wouldn't whale on us like he had with the eighth grader, Carlos? That he would punish our class with more compassion, weird as that sounds?*

I still didn't trust him.

The next week, Joseph Connelly, one of six white boys in our class of thirty, became the second casualty. He had forgotten his homework also.

"But I did do it, Brother. I really did."

"Come get your medicine, Joseph," Brother Steven said, in what would become his favorite prepaddling phrase.

Joseph got into position, and Brother Steven swung his paddle. But before he could connect, Joseph convulsed and collapsed on the floor. We cracked up again. Brother Steven grinned and actually winked at us.

"Let's try this again," he said.

This time Brother Steven purposely stopped his paddle in midswing, and Joseph performed the same routine, falling into a heap like he was having a seizure.

Take three: Brother Steven held Joseph by the back of his jacket and hit him fairly softly. Joseph smiled proudly and winked at Chino as he walked back to his seat.

"No big thing," Joseph said.

Not every subsequent punishment was a sketch comedy, but by and large, our class treated getting hit as fodder for snaps and goofing: "Hey, Joseph, you looked retarded up there," or "Yo, Roberto, you turned so red you looked like a Goya bean."

This making fun of beatings was, I see now, a form of self-preservation common among victims of violence, like when Richard Pryor joked about his grandmother making him get the stick she was going to beat his ass with or his father telling him to stand in the middle of the road while he started the car. You laughed because it *was* funny—and because you survived it.

It was hard to be funny when humiliation was involved, however. One time, Brother Steven hung this kid Gregory on a coat hook next to the blackboard. Gregory had arrived late for class, and Brother Steven had lifted him off his feet and pinned him on the hook. For an extremely long minute, Gregory dangled like a marionette while Brother Steven continued teaching. A few of us broke out laughing, but Brother Steven's steely stare silenced us.

"It's not funny, is it, Gregory?" Brother Steven said, without looking at him.

"No, Brother."

"Correct. It is not."

We snapped on Gregory afterward, of course, and he laughed at himself too. But I could tell that Gregory was really embarrassed—and pissed. Brother Steven had crossed a line.

For my part, I kept my streak of straight A's alive and never got hit. I even won the school's Medal of Excellence a couple of times, a gold pin engraved with an image of Jesus Christ. The first time I received the award, my friends ranked on me.

"David's a doofus!" Julio said.

"Brainiac is now a pussy, too!" Chino added. And on it went.

Eventually I goofed on myself, even to the point of calling myself Birdbrain, which was a stupid thing to do. Brainiac at least had a ring to it.

But my defensiveness about being a top student was starting to grow, at least among my close friends. It was different with the other high scorers in class, guys like Jose Gonzalez and Patrick Enright. We saw report cards as a form of competition, friendly most of the time, but streaked with envy when someone's grade average just beat the other one out.

"What'd you get, Dave?" Jose would say.

"A 95."

"No fair! I got a 94."

"Close doesn't cut it."

"We'll get you next time," Patrick would add.

These conversations never went beyond a trading of boasts, however. I never hung out with guys like Jose and Patrick, never went to their houses to talk about science and history, never, in fact, saw any of them on the playgrounds. To my knowledge, I was the only school-smart guy from our class who also hung out.

I wasn't really *street* smart, though, and I wanted to be. That meant becoming both cool and tough—in short, a man. So while I was relieved to have avoided Brother Steven's fondness for hitting, a part of me envied the guys who did get tagged. To my young eyes, they belonged to an exclusive club of outlaws, like convicts who had done hard time. It got to a point that whenever they got pummeled, they would brag afterward that they "took it like a man."

Being the class bookworm, I now wondered: *Would I ever take it like a man?*

SEVEN

"*Lenguas Sabrosas*"

"And these are testicles, what some of you call 'balls,'" Brother Steven said, his pointer on an anatomical chart.

Muffled laughter, which Brother Steven accepted with good nature. "Okay, boys, settle down."

Circling the "balls," he continued: "Testicles are where sperm are stored. When released, they travel to the ovaries—here." He pointed to an adjacent chart illustrating the inner workings of female sex.

"God willing, your sperm will impregnate your wife's egg when she is fertile. And I stress the word *wife*."

Continuing his voyage, Brother Steven directed our riveted attention to the area underneath the birth canal. "This is where, um, babies emerge." Brother Steven didn't say that this was what we called "pussy," but I suspected he knew the term well.

"And that's the human reproductive process—a holy one, I should add," he said, wrapping up the lesson. The word *holy* produced more laughs.

"So are there any questions?"

Not a hand shot up. This was one area you didn't ask questions about, for fear of sounding childish or, worse, inexperienced with the *holy* reproductive process.

"Well, fine," he said.

When Brother Steven talked to us about sex, his entire manner changed. There was an added softness to the voice, a subtle yet noticeable faraway look in his eyes, as if his mind drifted somewhere else.

As he put away the chart, Father Kelly, one of the half-dozen priests in St. Luke's, strode into our classroom. "I have an announcement for the young men," he said to Brother Steven.

"Of course, Father. Boys, your attention please!"

Father Kelly was an intense priest, with thin lips and wolf-like gray eyes that somehow sparkled with compassion, even as they bored a hole into you. Father Kelly spoke to us the same way he celebrated Mass: solemnly.

"For those of you who want to serve St. Luke's, we need some new altar boys. It's a wonderful calling. I was an altar boy myself, and it made me grow. If anybody's interested, and I'm certain many of you are, please join me tomorrow after school in the church. Three o'clock. Prompt. God bless you all."

Father Kelly thanked Brother Steven, executed a military about-face and left. I looked at Roberto, who was grinning like the Cheshire Cat.

"Perfecto," he whispered.

"What?" I whispered back.

"I'll tell you later."

During recess, Roberto was full of energy. "Altar boy's the way to go!" he exclaimed. "You get to miss class if they give you the 8:45 morning Mass, and there's another Mass at noon! I'm joining."

Roberto always spoke like a guy in a hurry, his words straining to keep pace with the thoughts racing in his brain.

"Miss class?" Julio said. "Shit, sign me up."

"There's no weekday Mass at twelve," I said. "What's so exciting about being an altar boy, anyway?"

Roberto put his arm around my shoulder.

"Dave, check this out. Forget missing Mass. The *reason* to be an altar boy is that you get to give Communion to the girls. You get to see their tongues!"

Roberto paused for theatrical effect. I stared at him and shook my head.

"That's the weirdest thing I've ever heard."

"Now I'm really joining!" said Julio.

"Roberto, you are one sick guy," I said.

"Hey, it's the way I am."

I thought about it. Sneaking peeks at girls is what we boys did, looking up their dresses, scoping the panties. Hmm, tongues?

The next day, eight of us reported for altar boy duty. We sat in the front pew of the church while Father Kelly listed the rules.

"As you know, Mass is no longer conducted in Latin, so you should only need a few lessons to learn your responses and various responsibilities."

"Aw, I wanted to learn Latin," Julio whined.

"You can still learn Latin, my son," Father Kelly replied.

"No, that's okay."

"As I was saying, the Vatican has decided that Masses should be conducted in the language of the parish, in our case English, except for the Sunday Spanish Mass. Therefore, it shouldn't be difficult to learn what you need to know. There are two altar boys for every Mass. I do the assigning, and I expect everyone to be here when they are told to be here. Is that understood?"

"Yes, Father Kelly!" we chorused.

"Welcome to the Altar Boy Society," Father Kelly said. "Now let us pray."

This is like Jackie Gleason joining the Raccoons, I thought.

Our lines proved easy to learn. The priest said, "The Lord be with you," and we responded, "And also with you." Other duties were more challenging, like remembering when to fetch the holy water and being at the ready to ring a set of three tiny brass bells. They gave a melodic jingle, like Christmas chimes.

"This is like that Hunchback dude," Julio said.

"I think he rang a church tower bell."

"Same thing."

Two weeks after rehearsals, I was given my first assignment. As luck would have it, I was paired with Roberto. Our Mass? Sunday, 10:00 a.m. Prime time. A full house and lots of girls.

Although we were nervous about our first Mass, our "Amen's" and "Now and forever's" were smooth, our genuflections crisp. I executed the chiming of the bells with confidence and finesse, timing the rings to the magical spells that transformed wafers of no-taste bread and cheap wine into the Body and Blood of Christ.

Come Communion time, we were pumped. Roberto and I accompanied Father Kelly to the marble railing separating the altar from the pews. In front, the faithful formed two lines, ready to kneel and receive the Holy Eucharist.

The procession of tongues began. I marveled at their sheer variety. The best belonged to the prettiest girls. Roberto called them "*lenguas sabrosas.*" Sandy, an eighth-grade bombshell with a beauty mark near her *bemba* lips, had a tongue that reached so far it threatened to lick the Communion plate. Miriam, her skin as copper as a fried *chuleta*, unfurled a tongue glistening with saliva. I thought she would drool all over her low-cut peasant blouse.

I knew I was peeking at an intimate part of their bodies. That the girls were kneeling as I stood above them added to my fantasy. I imagined their delicately spoken "Amen's" directed at me. *Yes, David says, "Amen" to you, too.*

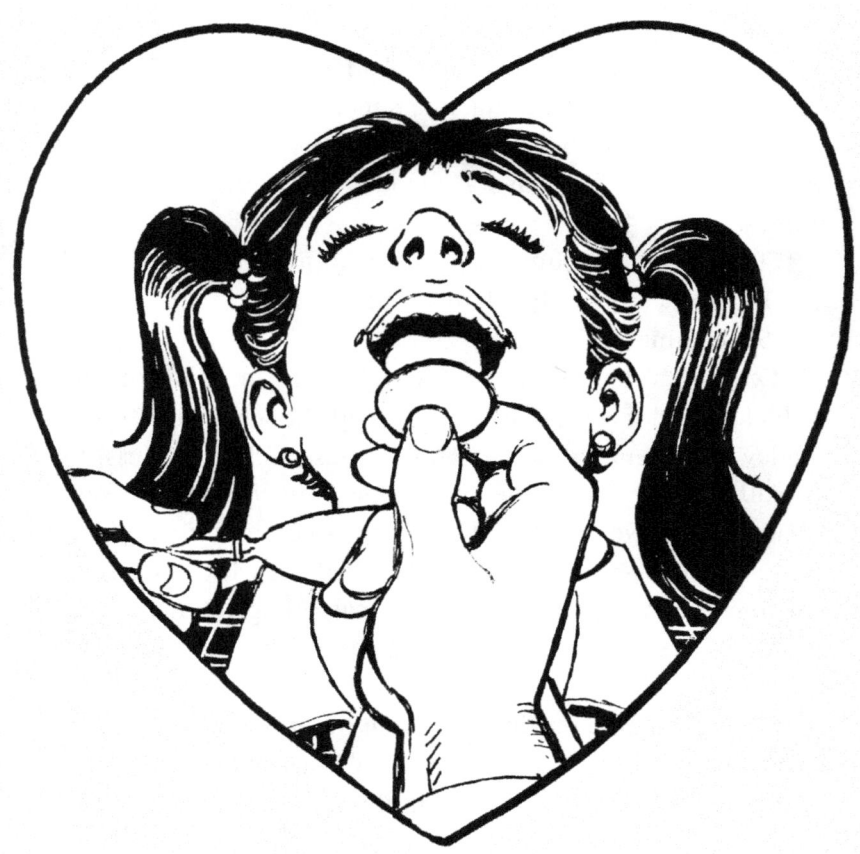

And did I mention cleavage? One busty girl looked up at me after taking her wafer, smiling knowingly as she crossed herself. I felt a stirring in my Fruit of the Looms and barely kept a straight face.

Outside, after Mass was over, Roberto slapped me five. "What'd I tell you, bro'? What do you say now?"

"I say hallelujah!"

EIGHT

Christmas Cribs

As seventh grade rolled in, the news was that Brother Steven had left St. Luke's. No one knew whether he had left the school or the brotherhood entirely. In the absence of hard facts, rumors swirled: that Brother Steven had enlisted in the Marines, that the biology lessons had made him see the light and become a free-love hippie.

Chino invented his own reason: that Brother Steven was tough, but we were tougher. After having us as students, he simply couldn't go on. I liked Chino's version and imagined myself as part of the tough crew that had forced Brother Steven to surrender to our might and will.

"We're just too bad!" I crowed, not really believing a word of it.

Whatever the reason, Brother Steven was history. Next up: Brother Lawrence.

Brother Lawrence had Raisinet eyes set in a cookie-dough face, his skin flaky. In the classroom, he paced like a caged animal. One crisp Monday morning early in the school year, the beast was sprung.

Brother Lawrence was in the middle of teaching fractions when the intercom in the back of the classroom rang. He picked up the earpiece, leaned into the speaker and began chatting with Brother Raymond, warden of the Boys Department at St. Luke's.

"Top of the morning to you, Brother Raymond…yes, we received the math textbooks…yes, some are missing pages…I can't hear you, what?"

While the brothers talked shop, we began talking, too. It started in low whispers, but soon we were bustling and laughing. Brother Lawrence slammed the intercom receiver down, his face a raw steak.

"I couldn't even *hear* him!"

Spittle and dandruff flying, he sprinted to the blackboard and grabbed his paddle—a chunk of polished wood not much smaller than a two-by-four. Starting alphabetically with Sammy Acevedo in the first row, Brother Lawrence went up and down the aisles, smacking each of us in the back.

I remained motionless, unable to grasp that he was actually hitting *everyone*. A few guys tried to crawl under their desks, which only pissed off Brother Lawrence more. Using his free arm as a crane, he hoisted the cowards by their shirt collars, plummeted them back into their seats and hit each twice.

When Brother Lawrence got to yours truly, I hunched my back in anticipation. *Bam!* came the paddle between my shoulder blades. My wool jacket absorbed most of the blow, but it still stung, a burning sensation that wound its way down my spine.

So this is what it feels like, I thought. *It must really hurt on the ass.*

By the time he reached a quivering Julio in the last row, Brother Lawrence had run out of steam. The paddle barely made a thud on Julio's back.

Julio exhaled with relief.

It was hard to imagine how the rest of the class could proceed after *that*. But these Brothers of the Sacred Heart were well trained. Brother Lawrence wiped his brow and stared at us, as if to say, "You got a problem with me?" He gently placed his weapon on the desk, picked up his math textbook and said, "Let us resume."

And we, desperate for a return to sanity, began scribbling away in our composition notebooks about "the common denominator."

"Sick puppy," Julio said afterward, shaking his head.

"Try psycho," I said.

"That shit didn't even hurt," Chino said and began shadow boxing.

"Man, that's the first time I ever got hit," I said.

"We *all* got it, Dave. It doesn't count. You're still a Brainiac—and a pussy."

❖ ❖ ❖

Brother Lawrence mellowed considerably as fall semester chugged along. Except for the time he tossed Chino down the bleacher stairs during gym class—who bounced up with an "Is that all you got?" look—our troubled teacher kept his demons in check. He taught with vigor and enthusiasm, especially about world history and war, which went together, I learned.

As Christmas drew near, Brother Lawrence gave our class an assignment.

"You are to construct a recreation of the Nativity," he said, rocking on the balls of his crinkled cordovan shoes. "You can employ whatever materials you like. It can be metal, wood or perhaps moldable clay. You can use paint, even crayon. I want you to be imaginative, to place yourself in Bethlehem. Yes, Julio?"

"Is this like our science project?"

"No, this is your *Christmas Crib Project*. Today's the first of December, so you have two weeks to finish this assignment. But please do not wait until the last minute. I want to see effort! And I assure you boys, you *will* be rewarded. Yes, David?"

"What kind of reward?"

"I'm not going to tell you. But you will be pleased. And I will be pleased. And most of all, God will be pleased."

For the next couple of days, questions about the Christmas Crib Project made the recess period rounds: "Were Romans in the barn too?" "Does it matter what size box we use?" "Can we place the Nativity scene in a ghetto?" None of us gave detailed information about our plans. We carefully guarded our secrets, our personal Manhattan Projects.

George came up with the brilliant idea of using Silly Putty. When pressed on comic book pages, Silly Putty absorbed the images, which could then be stretched into different sizes and shapes.

"Who's going to be Mary?" I asked.

"Maybe we can find someone from *Prince Valiant*," George replied.

"Oooh, how about Dr. Strange for one of the Three Kings? And Odin for God?"

"God wasn't at the Nativity, Dave."

"He could be, you know, like a symbol, maybe. I mean, God is everywhere, right?"

"Let's think about it," George said. "I mean, Odin does have a white beard. Anyway, we're definitely going to need animals for the barn. I think sheep were there."

"And a camel," I reminded him.

We laid out our plans like we were reconstructing the Battle of Normandy, making maps of where to get grass and dirt, going on shopping expeditions to search for plastic animals and possibly Baby Jesus himself. George suggested we use some of our Christmas tree decorations and cover the manger in tinsel garlands and silver icicles.

"Too stupid," I said.

"Then what about a moat?"

"Perfect!"

A few days passed and I had yet to put together my Nativity scene. The ideas had become so elaborate that I felt paralyzed with indecision. I was able to get grass from the park, but where in the South Bronx could I find bales of hay?

Then one morning, without explaining why, Brother Lawrence erased the due date on the chalkboard and made it three days earlier. *Why did he do that?* I wondered.

Staring at the new date for a moment, Brother Lawrence hastily erased it and put back the old one. Growling, he erased it again.

This was just too much.

"'Scuse me, Brother Lawrence, why do you keep changing the date?" I asked.

Okay, so I asked the question without being called on. Yes, there was a *slight* tone to my voice. But, God as my witness, nothing I said warranted Brother Lawrence's reaction.

"Why are you *asking* me that?" he shrieked.

Brother Lawrence bolted to the dreaded blackboard ledge and seized his paddle.

Oh, no, don't tell me.

He glared at me, nostrils heaving.

I can't freaking believe this, is he really going to...

Brother Lawrence came at me with startling speed. To ward off the incoming attack, I raised my left arm, which was holding a copy of our current book assignment, *What You Should Know about Communism and Why*. Brother Lawrence flung aside my puny shield and hit me on my arm. Twice.

Astonishment? Bewilderment? Not even close. This was *The Twilight Zone*, another dimension of space, time and mind.

I picked up my book about the evils of Godless Russia and smoothed its battered front cover.

"Any more questions, David?" Brother Lawrence huffed.

"No, Brother," I muttered, massaging my bruised limb, as well as my superbruised ego. Here, I finally get hit, finally get singled out for discipline, and it's all because I asked a simple question about a bullshit Nativity project.

As expected, my friends had a field day after school, snapping on how ridiculous I looked cowering in my seat with a paperback book to fend off the onslaught.

"The mighty shield of David!" Julio yelled, displaying my ruined book.

"Oooh, please don't hit my other arm," added Roberto.

"Brainiac gets whacked like a pussy," said Chino.

"Hey, at least I took it like a man!" I said, which elicited more howls of laughter.

❖ ❖ ❖

At home, I told a visibly disappointed George to forget our elaborate plans for the Nativity.

"No Silly Putty?" he pouted.

"Nah, let's just use Play-Doh. I don't care anymore. Brother Lawrence gets me so mad sometimes."

I related the bizarre episode to my brother, who had had Brother Lawrence the previous year.

"He's tormented," George explained.

"Well, the hell with him."

We constructed the Nativity without passion. I molded the Play-Doh into shapes somewhat resembling people, while George drove toothpicks into the dough to make eyes and ears. A slicing motion from a butter knife created mouths. I sculpted two pitiful-looking sheep and adorned them with gauze pads. My lone camel was barely recognizable, more like a dog with humps. Two shoeboxes glued together became the manger. We completely abandoned the moat idea.

From the bedroom closet, I fished out the thumb-sized pink plastic baby I had bought from the party favors section of Woolworth's.

"Was Baby Jesus pink?" George asked.

"He is now," I said.

Our class unveiled the secret creations in the St. Luke's cafeteria. It being a school day, only a few parents attended. My mother was busy with holiday shopping, but she had already seen my work.

"You got lazy, *mijo*," she'd commented.

As it turned out, there were *no* prizes for Best Nativity Scene. Brother Lawrence told our class that the "appropriate" reward was the knowledge that we were all "winners in God's eyes."

My Christmas Crib Project got mixed reviews. Clever for the live grass and dirt in the manger, dumb for the Play-Doh and the sickly sheep. No one was able to identify the camel.

Julio came up to me. "What happened, Dave? You constructed it this morning?"

"I stopped giving a shit," I whispered to him.

Julio patted my back in appreciation. Besides taking it like a man, "not giving a shit" was yet *another* sign of cool, a mark of youthful rebellion and snubbing your nose at authority.

"I'm proud of you, man," Julio said.

"Thanks, bro'."

Julio then showed me his handiwork. I had to hand it to him. Julio had simply cut out Nativity pictures from magazines and glued them to the inside of a box.

"Wow!" I said.

Christmas Eve that year was the usual brand of chaos. Cousins from Puerto Rico I saw only on the holidays came to our apartment by the boatload and ate our hard-earned mounds of food. Holidays were the only time of the year Mami prepared *pasteles*, a tamalelike delicacy made by grating green plantains into *masa*, which is then stuffed with pork, recao leaves, garbanzo beans and olives (among other items), wrapped in banana leaves, tied with twine and boiled in salted water for at least one hour. It was an extremely labor-intensive process, but the result was heaven on earth.

Pops honored Christ's birth by making *coquito*, a rum and coconut brew that smelled like sweetened rubbing alcohol. The adults loved it, chasing their drinks down with beer.

The Nativity project over and done with, I looking forward to altar boy duty at the Christmas Eve Midnight Mass, a colorful extravaganza that lasted two hours plus and included the processional Cross, two incense braziers, three priests, four altar boys and the pièce de résistance: a statue of the Baby Jesus. It also promised a slew of girls dressed to the nines receiving Communion.

In the kitchen Mami was boasting about her son, the altar boy. For Puerto Rican households, altar boy service was a veritable precursor to priesthood, something you showed off at family gatherings. Of course, Mami hadn't a clue as to why I had really joined. Nor did George, who had become more serious about Catholic duties. He was currently the St. Luke's sexton and a member of the church choir.

"David, *venga aqui*," Mami said, waving me into the smoke-filled kitchen. She was puffing on a Parliament.

"Having your annual cigarette, Mami?"

"*Ay si*, and my beer, too. I'm being, how do you say, naughty."

That cracked up the other women in the kitchen, all of whom were also smoking and drinking. Ah, the Christmas spirit.

"Yes," Mami continued, slurring a bit, "I got my *pasteles*, my two boys, my family. Friends. Health. So far, so good."

Our next-door neighbor, Juanita—whom we called Kitty, as in *Gunsmoke*'s Miss Kitty—gave me a bear hug. Like her husband,

Oscar, Kitty was no slouch when it came to guzzling liquor. Their three kids—Sunny, Raymond and Gladys—were quite the trio too, each of them with a streak of mischief that bordered on mayhem.

"So, David, you're a goddamn altar boy!" Kitty said, belting down another shot of *coquito*.

"Yeah, I'm doing the Mass tonight."

"No snow tonight."

"Back home, we never have white Christmas," Mami added. "No cold either."

This led to a back-and-forth debate over which was better: New York or Puerto Rico, jobs or climate, living among various nationalities or sticking to your own kind, modern plumbing or shitting in the outhouse.

The latter always struck me as weird. Who the hell wouldn't want flushing toilets? Whenever our family visited the island, we stayed with Mami's side of the family, in the house she grew up in, perched precariously on a hill on supporting wooden beams that looked like oversized stilts.

Abuela's home had an outhouse that was absolute misery: I had to squat to shit into a chamber pot, enduring the buzzing of mutant flies with giant emerald heads, wincing at the moist plop of caca on metal, wiping myself rapidly to end the ordeal. Afterward Abuela would always greet me with a smile.

"*Pobre nieto*," she would say with a hearty laugh.

In time, Abuela upgraded to an outhouse with a toilet seat and a hole. But the flies remained. Still, simple country living did have its beauty. I loved looking at the lush lime-colored hills of Caguas, feeling the sensation of expanse as I played in the fields, practicing my diminishing Spanish and getting an instant tan. But, for now, city living was the place for me.

The clock read 11 p.m. "I have to go to Mass soon, Mami. Can we open up our presents?"

"Yes, let's do."

We went back to the living room, where Pops and his buddies were singing *décimas* at the tops of their lungs, as if to impress the entire eleventh floor. Mami waited until Pops finished his song, something about the poor always having to suffer while the rich enjoyed life.

"Jorge, let's open George and David's presents," Mami said.

"Now?"

"They have to go to Mass."

"Now?"

"David's the altar boy and Papo has to sing."

"He can sing with us."

Pops said okay and grabbed two boxes from under the Christmas tree, adorned with so much tinsel, angel hair, ornaments and lights that there was barely any green to be seen. The other kids in the house started screaming to open their presents too, but were shushed by their parents and told they had to wait until midnight.

I tore open my package first. It was Captain Action, a comic book action figure who came with separate costumes that allowed him to change into Spider Man, the Lone Ranger and Flash Gordon. My Captain Action wore his traditional blue and black uniform, with lightning sword and ray gun.

"All right! This is exactly what I wanted. Thanks!"

"Now you go, Papo," said Pops.

"Out of the way, Chiquitín," George said as he unwrapped his gift and revealed a tape recorder. "Oh, this is so neat!" he said, hugging our parents.

The adults immediately began an excited chorus of "Oooh, let me tape myself!" and "Wait, I want to sing!" All of a sudden I felt like a little kid, my Captain Action forgotten in the rush of relatives jockeying to be among the first to have their voices recorded, fascinated with this portable wonder of technology.

I had no idea George had wanted a tape recorder, and for the first time I felt our age difference. We were separated by slightly less than a year. But at that moment we might as well have been born a decade apart. George had wanted a grown-up present. I had wanted a toy.

I took Captain Action and had him look out the window with me. Through the maze of Christmas lights and our blinking Santa Claus, countless windows winked back from the projects across from ours. To the south of my building, the murky waters of the Harlem River flowed like an overturned ink bottle. Beyond the river was the skyline of Queens.

George came up to me. "We should leave now, Dave."

As we put on our coats, George said, "You won't believe this, Dave, but I like your Captain Action. Maybe we can trade playing with our presents later."

"Really?"

"Sure. But just remember that it's *my* tape recorder."

❖ ❖ ❖

I arrived at the sacristy around 11:30 p.m. The other altar boys were already there: Julio, a classmate named Melvin—the first Puerto Rican I knew with red hair and freckles—and a pious sixth grader named Pablo.

Father Kelly was also there, putting on his vestments alongside Father Ignacio, freshly arrived from Spain. The two priests were yakking it up with Father Ryan, the new pastor at St. Luke's, having replaced Monsignor Mulcahey, who had died the previous year, in 1966. Father Ryan was a rather hip priest who donned a beret and love beads when prowling the streets of the South Bronx looking for souls to save. In time, he would let his hair and beard grow and become the longest serving pastor in the Archdiocese of New York.

"We're going to welcome some of the parishioners," Father Ryan said to us as he adjusted his satin sash. "You boys need to be ready in ten minutes."

The trio left the room, leaving the four of us to finish preparations, part of which entailed tucking Baby Jesus into a makeshift bassinet, complete with soft cotton blankets and straw.

I peered into the pseudocrib. The porcelain infant stared back at me with vacant blue eyes and chubby cheeks buffed to a scarlet glow. Spooky.

Julio came over, picked up the statue and began rocking it back and forth, cooing, "Rockabye, Jesus, on his sweet crib…"

"Quit messing around," I said. "Put the baby down."

Julio continued cradling the statue.

"This is blasphemy!" roared Pablo.

Julio added some mambo steps to his moves and spun the statue around in his hands. It hit the wall, breaking Baby Jesus's left foot at the ankle.

"Holy shit!" Melvin yelled.

"Holy shit!" I echoed.

"You can't curse in the sacristy," Pablo said, stricken. "Oh dearest God, what are we going to do?"

"Hey, Saint Pablo, relax. We'll fix this," I said.

Jesus, what is it about freakin' Christmas cribs? I muttered to myself.

A small closet in the sacristy housed some basic tools and cleaning supplies. Melvin pilfered inside and came out with a plastic jar filled with screws and nails.

Pablo gasped. "You're going to put *nails* in *Jesus*?"

"Forget that," I said, opening a desk drawer. "I found some Scotch tape!"

"It's a miracle!" Pablo said.

As the other guys looked on, I wound a good two yards of tape around the statue's severed ankle. It worked, sort of. The tape was visible and not very adhesive; Jesus's foot dangled.

"We better wrap the blanket around him," I said.

Just then Father Kelly materialized out of nowhere. We froze and stood in front of the bassinet, shielding Baby Jesus. Melvin clutched the cotton blanket in his hands.

"Boys, are you sweating?"

"Yes," Julio croaked.

"We're just about to put the blanket on our beloved Savior," Pablo said.

Father Kelly approached us. "Step aside."

We parted like the Red Sea as Father Kelly floated toward Baby Jesus's bassinet, eyes widening in mounting horror. "Who committed this...this *desecration*?"

I looked at Julio. Julio looked at Melvin. Pablo looked toward heaven.

The wall clock ticked off seconds, which echoed loudly in the room. Finally, Julio snapped. "I did it, Father. But it was an accident, I swear."

"Do not swear! You are to change into your regular clothes immediately and leave. Do you hear me?"

Julio began trembling and looked like he was going to cry. I felt sorry for him and kind of bad for the statue, too. It was one thing messing with a toy from Woolworth's like in my Christmas Crib Project. This rosy baby was actually blessed with holy water.

Julio shuffled his feet.

"I said leave! Right now!" Father Kelly commanded.

Julio flung off his altar boy outfit in one seamless move, running out the door and almost bumping into Father Ryan and Father Ignacio as they reentered the sacristy.

"What's the matter with Julio?" Father Ryan asked, looking at us all with suspicion.

Father Kelly carried the defiled statue over. "Julio claims it was an accident, but I wonder about that!"

Father Ryan looked at the damaged goods and shook his head. He took Baby Jesus and handed him to Father Ignacio, who said, "*Ay bendito, mira lo que pasó a Jesús Cristo.*"

"*Si, es malo,*" Melvin said in an atoned voice.

Father Ignacio grabbed the blanket from Melvin and wrapped it lovingly around the statue. He placed the swaddled Savior atop the strands of straw.

"I'm disappointed in you, Pablo," Father Ryan said to our sixth grade holy boy. "You told me you want to be a priest!"

"I do, Father," replied Pablo, practically in tears. "This wasn't my fault. I told Julio to stop, I really did."

What a punk, I thought. In my neighborhood, it was a cardinal rule never to tell on each other. If there existed a South Bronx version of the Ten Commandments, "Thou shalt need not be a punk" would be on the top of the list.

"I'm disappointed in you too, David," Father Ryan added. "I thought you were a smart boy."

"I am, Father Ryan. I do good in school *and* I'm on the track team."

Father Kelly strode over. "Well, you're no longer on the *altar boy team!*"

I bowed my head and got ready to sulk when it hit me: I was getting kicked out of the altar boy's club. Actually *expelled* from something. How cool was that!

I sulked anyway, to placate the angry fathers.

"Well, let us forget this for now," Father Ryan continued. "We need to start Mass. We are celebrating the birth of our Savior; let this be a joyous day."

"Amen!" I yelled, drawing a glare from the three priests.

Christmas Midnight Mass went off without further incident. Hundreds of parishioners crammed the church, sitting and kneeling and standing and reciting hymns and giving generously when the wire baskets were passed in front of them for money for St. Luke's and the poor box.

I glanced up at the balcony, where George was singing merrily, merrily along with his fellow choir members. He actually had a pretty good voice, a deep basso that could hold a note.

As expected, Holy Communion was a smorgasbord of delightful tongues, the girls heaving their exquisite breasts as they gulped down the Body of Christ. I sighed in resignation, my hand over my heart as I held the silver plate under their precious chins. This was my last Mass as an altar boy. No more *lenguas sabrosas*, no more pranks in church, nothing that made religion fun.

But I did get to see Linda Ramos take Communion. I still considered her my girlfriend, even though I'd barely spoken to her since our stroll down the block after Confirmation. Watching her tongue unfurl like a lily pad rekindled my longing.

The joys of tongue gazing notwithstanding, I hungered to try the real thing, to "scheme out," as we called tongue kissing in my neighborhood back then. All my friends claimed to have schemed out at least once. I, of course, claimed the same thing—and not just once, but several times, with my tribe of cousins in Puerto Rico.

This was a convenient lie. Like most of my Puerto Rican friends, I boasted that our homeland was overflowing with kissing cousins, especially the countless country *jibaras* who wanted to experience the sweet mouths of their sophisticated New York City kin. Inside, however, I knew the truth: I was a kissing virgin, and I needed to do something about it.

In the space of one month, I had taken some crucial steps toward becoming a man. A demented teacher had hit me. Then I had graduated to "not giving a shit." Now I was getting expelled from a religious society.

But there was still one more step to take.

As Linda stood and walked back to her seat, I vowed: *One day,* mi amor, *I will taste that delicious tongue.*

NINE

First Date

"Youth Dance in the Cafeteria! Come Celebrate Spring! All Invited!" The poster, festooned in magic marker and glitter, was tacked to the bulletin board outside the school office. Roberto said that the youth dance was mostly for this year's graduates.

"This is like their prom night, Dave. Why, you thinking of crashing it?"

"Maybe," I said. "I mean, look: It says it's for *everybody*. I think it'll be fun."

"Well, you won't catch me at no school dance," Roberto said, running a comb through his small Afro. "I make my own parties, you know what I'm saying?"

None of my friends said they were going: too busy, a waste of time, other family obligations to attend to. But here was a dance my parents would have no problem letting me go to, something close by and undoubtedly chaperoned. Not that

I'd ever asked them. Before this, I had no interest in going to parties. Not that I'd ever been invited. But it was May, a good time for a youth dance: school winding down, summer love on the horizon, and me in desperate need of scheming out. After finally seeing my beloved Linda's full-of-promise tongue, my mind was made up: it was time to join the distinguished ranks of lover men.

A couple of days later, I ran into Linda at the Big Park. She was on the Big Swings.

"Hey, stranger," she said.

"Hey, Linda, how you doing?"

"Fine. Wanna push me?"

"Sure."

I pushed the swing gently. Linda swayed in the wind, pigtails like pendulums. I took a deep breath and went for it.

"So, Linda, I know we haven't seen each other in a while, but you wanna, you know, go to that youth dance at St. Luke's tomorrow night with me? I mean..."

"Yes, David, I'd love to."

"Yeah?"

"Yeah."

She said yes! And without hesitation! Now what?

Linda used her Keds to brake to a stop. "I really want to go, David."

"Cool," I said, wishing I could pump my fist in the air. "Are you okay with the dance being more for the eighth-graders?"

"Hey, that's even better. At least the music will be hip."

Hip!

"I'll pick you up tomorrow night, what, like around seven?"

"Groovy, David."

"Right on," I said, instantly hipper.

On my way home, I ran into Julio and Roberto, who were practicing stickball in the Little Park. "Yo, guys!" I yelled. "Guess who I'm taking to the youth dance?"

Roberto stopped in midpitch. "You're still going to that piece of shit?"

"Yeah, and I'm taking Linda Ramos!"

"She has nice freckles," Julio said.

"You're such a fucking moron, Julio," Roberto said.

"Well, I bet she'll have an even nicer tongue!" I said.

"Keep us posted, my man," Roberto said. "I want details. Hey, Julio, heads up. Here comes another fastball."

At home, Mami listened patiently to the sequence of events: the announcement of the dance, my need to go, and—drum roll, please—that her son had a date!

"A date? *Con quien?*" Mami asked.

"Linda Ramos. You know, the girl you met after Confirmation?"

"*Ay si, la muchacha buena.*"

"Yeah but the dance's tomorrow night so I need some dress clothes."

"*No tengo dinero.*"

"Aw, come on, Mami!"

"*Mijo.* I can't give you what I don't have."

"What about Pops?"

"I don't have because he don't have. Maybe after next payday we have. But today, no have."

I tried a different tack. "Okay, Mami, I understand. I don't really need new clothes." I gave her a hug and then pouted.

A pause. "Wait a second," Mami said and went to her bedroom. She returned with a ten-dollar bill. "Here, so my baby can look good."

I was about to protest. *Ten dollars?* What the hell could I buy with that? But I knew Mami was sacrificing. Ten dollars could buy a lot of rice and beans.

The following morning, I strolled down 138th Street between Brook and St. Ann's avenues, the main shopping strip in our neighborhood. As usual, the block was full of shoppers, most of them, like me, on the hunt for bargains.

Where I really wanted to go was King's Clothing Store ("Where the Customer Is King!"), whose display windows taunted me with the hippest of fashions: lavish alpacas, radiant sharkskin pants and plush Playboy shoes. The Playboys alone cost twelve bucks.

I sighed and went two storefronts down to Viceroy's, a clothing store that catered to people of modest income. With resignation, I chose a plain-looking yellow cotton dress shirt and charcoal pants with two percent mohair. For shoes, I settled for what I already had at home: a pair of black leather dress shoes with a fake lizard pattern etched into them. Chino called them "the unknown shoes."

Next up was a haircut, which Mami insisted I needed "to look *muy* handsome."

Julito's was on 137th Street, next to Joe's Candy Store, and was just as popular. When you walked in, a heady aroma of Aqua Velva, Vitalis and manly chatter greeted you, followed by Julito's booming, "*¡Bienvenido!*"

As I waited for my turn, I picked up a copy of *Look* magazine from the Formica side table. Underneath it was a copy of *Pimienta*. I placed the *Look* down and flipped open the *Pimienta*. Staring back at me in grainy black and white were pictures of a naked woman sitting on a rock alongside a beach. She looked happy.

"*¡Tu eres muy joven!*" Julito called out.

"*Yo sé,*" I said, putting the magazine down. What did he mean too young? I was going on twelve years old, almost a teenager!

Julito harrumphed and resumed clipping his customer's hair. I waited a few seconds and deftly slipped the *Pimienta* inside the *Look* magazine. Coast clear, I opened the magazine again and found my happy brunette. She was in profile, head tilted back in the sunshine, legs crossed at the ankles, nipples pointed toward the ocean.

First Date

That was not the first time I saw a naked woman. In Puerto Rico, I had peeked through a keyhole to watch my foxy-looking aunt take a bath. I must have been about seven years old. The water was running, and Mami was out on the patio. Squinting, I made out a flash of creamy buttocks and then a hint of black *cholcha* hair.

"Wow," I whispered. Then my mother called for me.

"Coming, Mami."

"David!"

This time it was Julito who broke my reverie. "You're next."

"Coming," I said.

I got on the barber chair. "I like *Look*."

"No, you like *to* look!"

❖ ❖ ❖

That evening, I stared at my reflection in the bathroom mirror. My normally straight nose had a slight bump on it from playing tackle football without a helmet. Kind of cool, I thought. Maybe I could invent where I got it from, some fight with a bigger guy who didn't know who he was fucking with. My brown hair was thick, slightly wavy and parted to the side with a dab of Brylcreem. I puckered my lips in a mock kiss, my broad bottom lip prominent. Inching toward the mirror, I opened my mouth and stuck out my tongue. It seemed a nice size, not overly fleshy. *It definitely has potential*, I thought.

In the living room, Mami inspected me carefully.

"My baby looks good."

"I'm not a baby, Mami."

"I know, *mijo*," she said, brushing lint from my navy blue blazer. She told me to be home by 10 p.m. Since that was Linda's curfew also, I didn't make a stink about it.

At seven o'clock, I arrived at Linda's seventh floor apartment and rang her doorbell. Her building, 620 East 137th Street, was exactly like all the others in the Millbrook Houses: red brick exterior, hospital-green interior, gunmetal elevator doors.

Linda answered the door. "Hi, David, you're right on time!" she said, quickly closing the door behind her.

"No hello to your parents?" I said.

"They're, uh, napping."

"Oh."

Linda wore a lemon dress that highlighted her curves and accentuated her coffee-colored hair, which cascaded down to the small of her back. Her eyebrows were in full bloom, a dark brown like maple syrup. Julio was right; Linda did have nice freckles, little dots that sprinkled her cheeks.

"You smell good, David," she said.

"I use Brut."

"Oooh, Brut, how manly."

"Hey, we're both wearing yellow!" I said, pointing to my shirt.

Linda smiled and looked down. "Nice shoes."

"Thanks. They're not real lizard, you know."

"I know. Well, I guess we should go, right?"

"Right!"

Even though it was early May, the warm evening air coated the streets like a blanket, the temperature already sixty degrees. Linda put her arm through mine, and my muscles instantly flexed, so they would appear harder than they were. She seemed not to notice (or care). We walked the three blocks to St. Luke's. The fronts of the bodegas were lined with people drinking Ballantine and Rheingold beer and playing dominoes.

Linda and I talked about music. She was a big Motown fan and really into James Brown. I listened to ABC Radio and loved all the Top Ten tunes.

"I can't wait to practice my moves with you!" Linda said.

All of a sudden my mouth felt as if I had swallowed chalk. There was a problem. I had never danced with a girl before. Did not know, in fact, if I could dance at all. Back at home in front of the bathroom mirror, I had shimmied and snapped my fingers and felt confident that my natural Puerto Rican–ness would somehow carry me through. That if all those couples on *American Bandstand* could shake, rattle and roll, then, by God, so could I.

But as Linda prattled on about how she "just loved to boogie!" my confidence sank. *What the hell was I thinking? Maybe I can fake a sprained ankle.*

We reached the St. Luke's cafeteria entrance. Teenagers in love mingled outside, a few of them tucked into corners, smoking cigarettes in the dark. We walked past the boiler room and into the youth dance. "Cool Jerk" was playing, and Linda sprang to life.

"Let's dance, David!" she squealed, steering me onto the dance floor.

"Already?"

"It's 'Cool Jerk'!"

I stumbled through "Cool Jerk." Linda must have been doing one of the latest dances, because the couple next to us was doing the exact same moves. I tried to copy whatever it was, but the effort made me more self-conscious. Linda flashed me a pity smile as I waved my arms up and down like a go-go dancer. Mercifully, the song was brief, and the crowd whooped as the DJ, whom everyone seemed to know, removed the 45 from the phonograph and searched for another hit tune.

"Cool song, right Linda? Get it, cool?"

"Uh-huh."

We sat on a lunch bench and drank fruit punch the color of ruby. Linda tapped her feet. I snapped my fingers and looked around, trying to see if I recognized anyone. The cafeteria was decorated with blue and pink crepe-paper streamers. Rainbow balloons camouflaged the ice chests and stacks of lunch trays. The tables had thick paper roll coverings that reminded me of a butcher shop.

I was the only guy from my class at the dance and the only one wearing a dress jacket. Bell-bottoms were the rage that evening, as were sharkskin pants in various colors. And stitch shirts. And Playboys. And everything else I didn't have.

"Stay in My Corner" by the Dells came on.

"Oh my God! We *have* to dance to this song!" Linda said and dragged me back onto the vinyl tile dance floor. Our bodies pressed together, and I melted, her breasts soft as cupcakes through her dress. My movements were still awkward, but I didn't care. I began humming the song in Linda's ear.

"Please don't do that," she said.

I noticed that Linda had moved her body further away, so that only our top halves were touching. Then I realized why. I had an erection. It deflated quickly.

Confidence back at zero, I walked her back to our bench when the song was over. I sipped from my Dixie cup and made an inane comment about Kool-Aid and piss. Linda grimaced and said I was gross. Normally, being called gross was something I would be proud of, a sign of boyish cleverness and wit. Not this time.

Linda excused herself to go the bathroom. I wandered over to the food table and waded in on the Ritz crackers.

"How you doing, bro'?" said a voice next to me. It belonged to an eighth grader nicknamed Fuji because of his Fu Manchu–like mustache. I'd seen him at the handball courts in the Big Park, which was frequented by quite a number of the hip, older crowd who sported the coolest nicknames: Tarzan and his brother Cheetah, Hustler and Cookie Man, Little Angel and Big Angel. I often thought they should experiment with elaborate Indian names like He Who Runs with the Deer or Man That Talks to the Wind. Theirs would probably have been He Who Runs from the Cops or Man That Talks to Himself.

"I'm doing good," I said to Fuji, who rocked on his heels and almost fell over. He was obviously on something stronger than fruit punch.

"Do you dig the party?" he asked.

"I do."

Linda returned from the bathroom and interrupted our bonding. "Hi, Fuji," she said.

"Hey, Linda."

They know each other?

A cheer went up in the cafeteria as "Reach Out" by the Four Tops came on. A rush of bodies filled the dance floor.

"I love that song!" Linda shouted. *Jesus, is there any song she doesn't love?*

"Let's dance," Fuji said to her. He turned to me. "That cool with you, bro'?"

"Yeah, um, sure," I said, uncertain whether to feel good that Fuji had asked my permission or bad that Linda didn't even look at me. I grabbed another Ritz.

Fuji and Linda giggled their way onto the dance floor and began mixing their dance moves with flirtatious glances. At one point in the song they waved to me. I grinned and waved back, instantly feeling like a *pendejo*—a fool.

After the dance, Linda came over to me. "Man, that was great. Can you get me something to munch on, David?"

"Ah, sure. You want Ritzes or Cheez Doodles?"

"You know what, I'll just have a little bite of yours."

"Okay."

I held out the Ritz, and Linda opened her mouth. There was her tongue again, just as I remembered it, wide and pink and drenched with possibilities. I slid the cracker in slowly, and Linda took a bite. It was Holy Communion déjà vu.

"You forgot to say amen," I said.

"What?"

"Never mind."

I excused myself to go the bathroom and empty out the fruit punch. When I got back, I found Fuji and Linda dancing again, this time to a salsa record: "Vámonos Pa'l Monte" by

Eddie Palmieri. They waved to me again, and I waved back half-heartedly. I sat back on a bench and stared into nothing.

The remainder of the evening went by like a movie montage: Linda practicing her cha-cha with another eighth grader; me reassuring her that my ankle was feeling much better; Father Kelly laughing it up with the soon-to-be high school students and frowning at the girls wearing a new thing called miniskirts.

At 9:00 p.m., Linda said she wanted to go home.

"Good idea," I said. "Boy, those two hours just flew by, huh?"

"Never faster."

We left the youth dance and walked back to Linda's building in silence. I waited for Linda to hold my hand, but no dice. Passing Joe's Grocery Store, I noticed the same group of guys still playing dominoes.

"This just ain't my fucking night," said an old man in a Panama hat. "Losing, losing, losing."

You and me both, buddy.

When we got off the elevator in her building, Linda began walking down the hallway to her apartment. I stood rooted in front of the elevator door, my gaze on the tiled floor. Linda came back and, with her finger, pulled my chin up.

"Well, aren't you going to kiss me?" she said.

"Huh?"

"Don't you want to?"

I looked into Linda's dark brown eyes and envisioned swooping her in my arms like Rudolph Valentino amid a crescendo of violins. A voice inside of me screamed, *Go for it,* pendejo! *This is what the date was all about!*

But I couldn't. After all the altar boy fantasies, all the lies about scheming out with my adoring cousins, after all that and more, I simply could not budge—or speak. Yet I felt myself leaning forward a microinch, ready to kiss, wanting to kiss. A door down the hallway opened and closed, its metal hinges echoing in the stillness. Before I got up the nerve, the moment passed.

Linda began walking back to her apartment. "Good night, David," she said without looking back.

"Bye," I said, staring down at my unknown shoes.

❖ ❖ ❖

"So, you scheme out with Linda or what?" Roberto asked.

"What do you think?" I said, neatly avoiding the question.

"How about feeling her up?"

"Nah, we were in the hallway. I didn't want her mom to catch us."

Another nifty side step; at least the first part was true.

"My man!" Roberto said, slapping me five.

That morning, I had cooked up a fable about my miserable first date the night before. How Linda and I kissed for a long time and panted afterward, two starry lovers who couldn't get enough of each other. But it was really no big thing, I would crow, because I was already such an experienced kisser and accustomed to girls swooning over my charming ways and sweet lips.

But now that Roberto had begun his expected grilling, I discovered I didn't want to lie. Not for honorable reasons, mind you, like earning extra heaven points for being the only honest kid in the entire universe or being a refined caballero who values truth above all.

No, none of the above; I didn't want to lie because Linda might get wind of my bullshit and tell the whole block the wretched truth. She would snicker at my spastic dancing, ridicule me for not kissing her when I had the chance. And those shoes!

Still, I really couldn't be honest with my buddies. That would ruin me forever. With Mami, it was enough to say that I had a terrific time. That Linda was a good dancer and that she liked me. George didn't care one way or the other. Pops slept late and would be filled in later, if at all.

No such luck with Roberto. "You going to give me details, or do I have to beat them out of you?"

"I guess you'll have to beat me, because my lips are sealed. But my lips weren't sealed last night!"

Roberto slapped me five again. Mercifully, he stopped the interrogation and reviewed his hand of cards. We were in the Big Park playing Knuckles, a card game Roberto insisted was invented in Rikers Island Prison. I don't recall the exact rules except that the winner ended up with no cards and the loser got his knuckles hammered with the card deck.

"Damn, lost again," I said, balling up my left fist. Roberto administered the Slicer, which counted for five hits, or five losing cards. Instead of the usual rap on top of my knuckles, Roberto swung the deck's edge sideways, a slicing motion across the front of my knuckles that peeled skin. I stared at my slightly bleeding middle knuckle like it was a trophy. In the Millbrook projects, bruises and the drawing of blood equaled valor, especially when earned from games whose primary purpose was to inflict pain.

Chino joined us at the picnic table.

"Yo, Chino, you know that Dave went to the dance and got it on with Linda Ramos?"

"Who's Linda Ramos?"

"Does it matter who she is?" I said, eager to change the subject. "Besides, Chino, you told me you like public school chicks."

"They're easier," Chino said. "Don't got that guilt to deal with, all that Ten Commandments shit." This started an argument between him and Roberto, who thought Catholic school *jebas* were hotter because why else would their parents send them to St. Luke's if not to control their reckless lust?

I stayed out of the debate and continued to lose. This time

I finished with all fifty-two cards in my hand, which rarely happened.

"Oh, oh, Dave gets the Sandwich!" Chino said.

Roberto cackled, cut the deck and stood on the picnic table. I put my palm down on one of the deck halves as Roberto reached down and placed the other half on top of my hand, completing the hand sandwich.

"Here comes the *pilón!*" Roberto roared. He lifted his right foot and stomped the Sandwich" with his size 10 Converse sneakers. Hard. I stifled a yell and removed my trembling hand.

"Now you're a real man," Roberto said.

Chino was more cautious. "You're almost there, but you got to get rid of those fucking PF Flyers."

Jesus, me and my footwear!

Later that afternoon, Roberto and I went to the handball court to watch two of the older teenagers, Little Manny and Joe Mama, play a fierce game of handball.

Little Manny, future heroin addict with fair skin and blue eyes, barely broke a sweat and always seemed in the perfect position to hit the Spaldeen. Joe Mama, a mulatto with green eyes and a full beard, perspired so profusely that his chino pants were spotted in the crotch.

"That's one hairy dude," I said to Roberto.

"I got hairy nuts too."

"That's nice to know."

The handball game sizzled on. At one point, Joe Mama crouched low to counter one of Little Manny's relentless killers. A marijuana joint fell out of his shirt pocket. I'd never seen a joint before. I'd heard of them, of course. It was impossible to live in the South Bronx during the 1960s and *not* be exposed to drugs.

"That's a nice-looking j," Roberto said.

"A what?"

"A j. You never heard of that, Dave? "

"I know what a j is. I just didn't hear what you said."

"My cousin smokes herb," Roberto added.

"Smokes what?"

"Jesus, Dave, herb. It's what they call it too. I should take back what I said about you getting your hangout card."

"It's hard to keep up with the words sometimes."

Joe Mama retrieved his j, or herb, and told Little Manny that whoever won got to smoke it.

"Bet," Little Manny said.

Big Danny sauntered onto the court. A middleweight boxer, Big Danny didn't need to play Knuckles to prove his toughness. The previous summer, he had fought future Golden Gloves champion Eddie Gregory in a three-round exhibition bout organized by the New York City Fire Department boxing club.

Organizers had erected a boxing ring in the middle of the Big Park's basketball court. I stood alongside one hundred plus Blacks and Puerto Ricans and a handful of whites, a perfect reflection of the neighborhood. Hundreds more people were poking their heads out of the project windows. It was like a festival. The guy next to me was chugging down a quart of Colt 45 malt liquor, the growing beer of choice in the projects. In the near future I would guzzle the drink on a weekly basis, but for then I settled for an orange Popsicle.

Big Danny's bout was one of a series of fights that afternoon, and by the time he stepped into the ring, the crowd was pumped, whooping and yelling "Awright!"

A fireman introduced the two fighters.

"In this corner, fighting out of Brooklyn's Bedford Stuyvesant, we have Eddie 'The Flame' Gregory!"

Claps and hoots.

"And representing the Bronx, let's hear it for Danny Rivera!"

Cheers and whistles.

It was a case of boxer versus puncher, Big Danny using his left jab and footwork to avoid Eddie Gregory's power. Eddie got in a few solid shots, but Danny kept his cool and continued moving side to side. In round three, the two visibly tired warriors exchanged flurries, and the final bell rang. The bout ended in a draw, eliciting loud cheers from the spectators.

Eddie Gregory later became Eddie Mustafa Muhammad, the WBA Light Heavyweight Champion of the World.

Sitting in the handball court, I remembered my thrill at watching a live boxing match, the smack of leather on flesh as riveting as it was frightening. I didn't think—then and now—that I could *ever* do that. Of course, I wanted to, and my imagination played endless scenarios of me, twenty pounds heavier and muscled like Steve Reeves, beating the hell out of one hopelessly outmatched opponent after another. And yet I had never been into a fistfight. I wanted to think I'd never punk out, but I wasn't sure.

Little Manny won the handball game, 21 to 15. Joe Mama handed him the j.

"I'll smoke it later," Little Manny said.

"Aw, man, I wanted to smell the smoke," I said to Roberto.

"One day, that's gonna be us. Playing handball for some herb."

Big Danny came over. "One of you guys had next?"

"No, we were just watching," Roberto said.

"You're a good fighter," I added. "That was something last summer!"

Big Danny cracked his knuckles. "Losing was just out of the question, man."

When I left the Big Park, I looked back and saw none other than Linda Ramos walking into the handball court. Big Danny stopped playing, walked toward her and whispered something into her ear. Linda laughed.

A week later, as I was walking down 138th Street, I spotted them coming out of Woolworth's. They were holding hands.

Fuck!

TEN

Cons to the Rescue

I was depressed for days. My girlfriend-who-never-was had dumped me for a guy-I-could-never-become. And my friends knew it, too. Julio had also seen Linda and Big Danny together, and word had spread that David's girl had left him for a boxer.

Chino kidded me that we should "settle it in the ring." In between bouts of riding my ass, Roberto said it was all "part of the love game" and that I just had to say, "Fuck it."

Okay, I would say, "Fuck it." But what should I *do?*

The solution came as I sat in my bedroom, staring forlornly at my closet, mourning my sorry-ass wardrobe. My PF Flyers and unknown shoes were lined up like soldiers, mocking me alongside my other pair of nondescript black leather Tom McCann's that I wore a lot for school.

Footwear. There was that word again. And there, in a moment of revelation, the solution came.

Cons.

Cons to the Rescue

Everyone who was anyone owned a pair of Chuck Taylor Converse sneakers, white and low cut. The hip place to buy them was at Sam's Sporting Goods on 149th Street between Courtlandt and Morris avenues. You could also get them at Taylor's Shoes on 138th Street, which was only a block away from my apartment. But buying them from Sam's equated style—and showed that you had the extra dollar the sneakers cost there.

As luck would have it, I didn't have to beg like a leper to get the Cons. Pops had hit the numbers, so Mami readily agreed to buy me a pair. She did think that $7.95 was way too expensive for sneakers and reminded me how in *el campo en* Puerto Rico, people would wear one pair of shoes for everything.

"Yeah, Mami. That's why we live in New York."

"Yes, and you must always be thankful, no?"

"You bet."

So off I went to the Hub, the name given to the commercial area beginning at 149th Street where Willis, Third and Melrose avenues intersected. Still functioning at the time was the Third Avenue El, the overhead train that rattled between 149th Street and Gun Hill Road.

The Hub also housed *three* movie theaters: the Loews National, the RKO and the Bronx Theater, which at one time used to be the Bronx Opera House. Loews and RKO both showed first-run movies, with each feature preceded by a cartoon. The Bronx Theater showed three movies at a time for a dollar, second-rate flicks nobody had heard of, like *Monster A Go-Go* and *Manos: The Hands of Fate.*

When I arrived at Sam's, I inhaled the seductive aroma of leather, baby oil and resin. The store was a funhouse filled with crowded shelves of professional sporting equipment and clothes: baseball gloves and bats, footballs, basketballs, soccer balls and rows upon rows of sneakers, running shoes and cleats.

"Can I get a pair of Cons, white, low cut?" I asked the salesman, as if I ordered them all the time. He measured my feet, went to the back and came out with the world-famous red shoebox, the noble round logo with the Chuck Taylor signature prominent on the cardboard. He slid the sneakers onto my feet and tied the thick white cloth shoelaces. I stood up and walked around. They were a perfect fit.

This was not about sports. This was about statement, a limousine for the foot.

That evening, Mami surprised me by giving me more money for clothes. "Your father has been lucky."

It didn't bother me that the cash came from my dad's gambling. I didn't see it as a big problem, although that would soon change. And besides, my Mami seemed happy, so I was, too. It's like the joke in which the wife accuses the husband of having a gambling problem. The husband replies, "I just won a thousand dollars."

"Problem solved!" says the wife.

The next time around I was able to enter King's Clothing Store, where I purchased an elegant, dark green pair of sharkskins—not 100 percent sharkskin wool, but close—and a light brown stitch shirt. In the dressing room, I wanted to stare at my reflection forever, wishing I could have looked this way when I dated Linda. How different it would have been!

Pops was especially pleased that his winnings had given me what I wanted, but he still said, "All that money and only one pants and shirt?" He also thought it weird to wear sneakers with dress clothes. I assured him that this was the way it was done.

"How much you spend?"

"Twenty-five for everything."

"I buy a suit for that."

I showed George my new duds. "Check it out," I said. He grunted, agreed they were nice and went back to watching *Lost in Space*.

I waited for a Sunday Mass to make my grand public debut. Sunday Mass was *the* place to parade new apparel, especially during Christmas and Easter, when the church entrance was, basically, a catwalk.

Ditty-bopping up 138th Street to St. Luke's, I struggled to maintain a calm demeanor. It was absolutely vital to act like the clothes were "just a thing, my man."

Julio, Chino and Roberto were hanging out in front of the church.

"What's up, fellas?" I said, nonchalant.

"*Coño*, check out Dave with the Cons!" Roberto exclaimed.

Amazing how the sneakers were the first item to be acknowledged.

"And the stitch and the 'skins," Julio added. "And it ain't even a holiday. What's up with this, David?"

I took the accolades in stride, barely able to keep myself from leaping and cheering. Chino grinned and nodded his head. That said it all.

"It was just time," I said casually, slapping all of them five.

The church bells began ringing, the signal that Mass was starting. I strode up the marble stairs inside, saying hello to startled classmates and looking out of the corner of my eyes to see which girls were giving me the eye. I glimpsed Linda Ramos pointing at me and whispering something to a girlfriend.

Although I pretended not to notice, I ached to hear what Linda had to say. Regrets about not giving her ex-boyfriend another chance? That I was, in fact, a damn good kisser?

It was a nice fantasy—and no, it didn't count as a lie to be told in Confession. I received my Holy Communion feeling fresh again, having taken some important steps into the realm of cool.

ELEVEN

"Brother, I Can't Get Hit"

Eighth grade. Two brothers down, one more desperado to go: Brother Raymond, aka the "street fighter."

At least that's what Chino called him after once seeing Brother Raymond get into a brawl with a guy outside St. Luke's. "They were really going at each other," Chino told me. "I mean rolling-on-the-ground street shit, like two alley cats. The other dude was old, high school at least. When it was over, Brother Raymond got up, dusted off his robe, put his glasses back on and said, 'Ah, that was nice.'"

"What about the other guy?"

"He was like, 'Nice fight, man.'"

"So who won?"

"Nobody. They shook hands and that was that."

Chino couldn't remember exactly what the fight was about, something like the guy calling Brother Raymond a little punk. I thought I'd heard and seen it all at St. Luke's: nuns hurling chalk and wielding rulers, brothers pushing guys against walls and whaling on an entire class like they were carrying out a scorched earth policy. Now, it was a Brother of the Sacred Heart who enjoyed a good rumble.

I guess I shouldn't have been surprised. This was 1968, and the world was on fire. The Vietnam War raged on, as did demonstrations, marches and assassinations of civil rights and political leaders. Yet my buddies and I barely talked about what was detonating around us. A typical current events conversation went something like this:

Roberto: "Shit's getting crazy everywhere, man!"

Me: "Yeah."

Roberto: "Anyway, I'm hungry. Wanna go grab some *cuchifritos*?"

Me: "Hell, yeah."

I have no recollection of being stirred to anger. I did cry when President John F. Kennedy was assassinated in 1963, along with Mami and her best friend, Kitty, as we watched the funeral motorcade on television. When Dr. Martin Luther King, Jr., was killed in the spring of 1968, St. Luke's had a moment of silence, as they did when Robert F. Kennedy was gunned down two months later.

But overall, I didn't ask questions or seek answers. There was the world, and there was the Bronx. Or maybe I was just a kid with enough problems of my own.

Still, signs and symptoms of that tumultuous era were everywhere in my neighborhood. That summer of '68, a group of older teens faced off a few cops in the middle of 137th Street. I didn't know what started it, but the altercation escalated by the second, neither side backing down.

"Get off the streets now!"

"We *live* here, pig!"

"Move it!"

"Move us!"

As the tension mounted, Little Moses—a member of the Social Seven, the local gang whose symbol, a James Bond–like derringer, was painted on the handball court wall—emptied his quart of Colt 45 behind his back, ready to throw the bottle. I stood on the sidewalk alongside dozens of my neighbors, riveted to the showdown, ready to bolt if necessary.

But the situation was diffused somehow, and the crowd broke up. The cops from the local 40th precinct went back to their squad cars as the ready-to-rumble guys joked, saying, "Yeah, aha, that's right." Little Moses tossed his empty Colt 45 bottle in the trash.

"You pigs owe me a beer!" he yelled at the departing cars.

Not for the first time, I wondered if one day I could be that bold and fearless. As it turned out, I got to live out my imagination later that same summer, when a new playground game cropped up in Millbrook: Kill the Cop.

The rules were similar to Ring-a-Leevio. One person in the middle of the playground, the "cop," was "it." At one end of the playground, a group of three to five guys lined up in a safety zone. The cop's job was to catch them as they ran to the safety zone on the opposite end of the playground. If the cop caught you, he had to hold you long enough to say, "Kill the cop, one-two-three" three times. Then you became another cop. This went on until everyone was caught and became a cop.

Here's the rub: The cop(s) could also go *inside* a safety zone to make someone a fellow cop. But unlike when you're running from zone to zone, inside the zone the guy could fight the cop off with punches—roundhouse swings, left hooks, the works. There was no hitting the face, though, nor kicking the nuts. There had to be some rules! We had scruples.

The game was a godsend. While I had climbed several rungs of the ladder leading to manly cool, I'd yet to be in a fight, and Kill the Cop was the closest I got to actually trading blows. Well, mostly receiving them. I wasn't too good at fighting people off, but I was learning to take a good punch.

One time, I became a cop early in the game. Collis, the home run king of Off the Curb, taunted me to go into the safety zone and get him.

Collis was tall and skinny, with a dome head and bony knuckles. I went after him with gusto, getting punched repeatedly in my chest and arms. But I eventually got him in a bear hug and screamed, "Kill the cop!" three times.

"Hey, you can take it, man!" Collis said.

I considered that the highest possible compliment.

◆ ◆ ◆

It was within this atmosphere of rebellion and change that the stage was set for my final year at St. Luke's. Eighth grade would be high drama indeed.

Brother Raymond stood just over five feet tall, only a few inches taller than Mami. Yet every inch contained compressed hostility. He also played the melodica, a delicate instrument that was a cross between a harmonica and an accordion. On the first day of class he astonished me with a smooth rendition of "Amazing Grace." I half expected him to break into song afterward.

I knew, however, that the first few days of class were always insidiously deceptive, a lull before the storm. Sure enough, it wasn't long before Brother Raymond showed his true hand.

In the first humiliating episode, Joseph Connelly, the hapless white guy who was always being called on to do something, was summoned to the blackboard to figure out a math problem. Brother Raymond handed him a piece of chalk. Joseph weighed the problem and wrote the wrong answer.

"Try it again," Brother Raymond said.

Joseph stared at the problem for what seemed like an eternity, shaking, on the verge of tears. The overhead clock clicked loudly.

Joseph wrote another wrong answer.

Brother Raymond slapped Joseph across the face.

Joseph shook his head, as if refusing to cry. His left cheek was crimson, and I felt awful for him. This was a special type of brutality in a churning sea of brutalities. Slapping someone in the face in front of people is not about inflicting pain. It's about inflicting shame, which is far worse. Plus you just didn't hit someone in the face. Even in vicious games like Kill the Cop, the rule was no hitting to the face. If you did, it meant you wanted a real fight. It was a challenge.

Brother Raymond was challenging Joseph—and challenging us.

It took Joseph another slap to figure out the equation. He returned to his seat, quivering like he had stepped off the gallows. I glanced over at my classmate Richard. He was staring down at his math book, stone-faced as I was.

◆ ◆ ◆

In the seventh grade, Richard had asked me to help him with math homework. I said I would; it wasn't often a classmate sought my help.

Richard had a weird, innocent streak to him. One time he had telephoned me and asked, "Hey, David, you want to come to my house and watch my fishes?" I thought he was kidding but said yes, since he lived only two floors above me.

He wasn't kidding. We sat in front of his fish tank for thirty minutes and watched guppies and angelfish swim and eat fish food. I kept expecting a punch line, like Richard whipping out a piranha and tossing it inside. Nope, just fish watching.

When I arrived for homework help, Richard's mother greeted me. Her hair was wrapped in a tight bun, lips like pencil lines.

"Thank you for coming, David. Can I get you some milk and cookies?"

"That'll be nice, thank you."

"Richard just can't seem to understand decimals and fractions," Mrs. Morales said, a marked edge in her voice.

"Well, they can be hard sometimes."

Richard waved hey to me and we sat at the dining table, a salmon-colored Formica classic adorned with a ceramic bowl filled with fake fruit and a Felix the Cat salt and pepper shaker set.

Mrs. Morales set down a plate of Oreo cookies and a glass of milk. Richard opened his math book, his mother hovering behind him. He reached for an Oreo. "Not for you!" Mrs. Morales said.

Whoa. I took a bite of my Oreo, and we began. "Okay," I said, pointing to a sample problem. "Can you figure out how to put this into a fraction?" He wrote an answer on a scrap sheet of paper but got it wrong. "I don't get this stuff," he said. Mrs. Morales slapped him hard on the back of the head, a miserable thud that almost knocked off his glasses.

Richard swallowed and fought back tears. "Try again," Mrs. Morales demanded through clenched teeth.

It took me a few seconds to recover. My parents were sometimes strict, but nothing like this.

"You can do this, Richard," I said in a gentle tone, as if I were the caring mom.

Another wrong answer. This time Richard's mother slapped him across the face. Now the tears and mucus flowed. Shame enveloped me like a suffocating blanket. *How can a mother do this to her child right in front of me!* I wanted to take her Felix the Cat shakers and smash them but instead gulped down my milk in one long sip.

Richard didn't speak. He finally wrote the correct fraction, and we moved to another problem. Mrs. Morales straightened her apron and took my empty plate.

"Guess I'll go wash the dishes."

Somehow we got through the homework. I got up from the table and asked, "You want to watch the fishes together, Richard?"

He didn't, so I left.

❖ ❖ ❖

Maybe it was the accumulation of everything we had gone through with the Brothers of the Sacred Heart. Maybe it was the political environment encircling us. Maybe it was both. But the slapping of Joseph Connelly changed things. I could almost taste it: the sense of *basta ya*.

The first act of classroom insurgence involved Jose Rivera, whom we called Bob Hope because of his sloping nose. Looking back at his photo now, I see he looked nothing like the famous comedian.

Jose committed some minor infraction, and Brother Raymond grabbed his paddle (yes, he had one too) and told him to come outside. Like Brother Lawrence, Brother Raymond preferred to inflict his formal paddling in the hallway just outside the classroom. Opinions were mixed over why this was. The majority, myself included, believed that having the class hear only the crack of pine on ass induced its own special brand of terror (it did). Others wondered if perhaps it was the brothers' strange way of letting us salvage a little dignity.

Whatever the reason, Jose stood up, inhaled deeply and declared, "Brother, I can't get hit."

Brother Raymond was stunned, as was our entire class. Did we hear Jose right? That he *can't* get hit?

"I said, come outside."

"Brother, I can't get hit."

"Oh, you can't, eh?" Brother Raymond threw the paddle on his desk, flung off his wire-rimmed glasses, rolled up his sleeves, walked up to Jose and slapped him across the face.

"Brother, I can't get—" Another slap.

Jose squared his shoulders, inhaled and said his mantra again. And he was slapped again. Jose stood there, refusing to move. Brother Raymond gave up and told him to sit down.

That was the first time someone had said no to a Brother of the Sacred Heart, and it took willpower beyond words for me not to shout, "About fucking time!" My friends didn't see it that way, though. They snapped on Jose big time, saying that if he didn't want to get hit, then why did he let himself get hit?

"It was stupid," Chino said.

Jose defended his stance. "He wanted to use the paddle, and I said no to him. It's better than what you guys do."

"But he slapped you," Roberto insisted.

"That's right. And I still said no to him."

I asked the obvious question no one had raised. "Jose, *why* did you say you couldn't get hit?"

"I got a shot at the doctor's yesterday," he replied. "If I got paddled, it would've made it infected."

"Jesus Christ, Jose, why didn't you just tell him that?"

"It was none of his business."

Not long after that, more history was made. It involved Robert Tisdel, a newcomer to St. Luke's who liked to be called by his last name.

Brother Raymond was standing over Tisdel, screaming at him about constantly arriving late. Tisdel sat there, arms folded across his chest, his face saying: *And this is a problem because…?*

Brother Raymond slapped him across the face, and Tisdel shot out of his seat. "Don't you ever hit me again!" he thundered.

Tisdel pushed past Brother Raymond, almost knocking him over, and stormed out of the classroom. Brother Raymond remained motionless for a full minute, unable to wrap his oval head around this unprecedented act of mutiny. He readjusted his glasses and sat down. Another minute passed…maybe. I really don't know. I had lost all sense of time at this point. The bell rang; School was over for the day.

After class it was bedlam.

"Did you *see* that?" I said, pacing in the schoolyard. "Did you see what Tisdel did? Can you believe what goddamn Tisdel *did*?"

"This is a superbugout, man," Julio said.

"And did you see the look on Brother Raymond? He didn't even say anything to him when he walked out!" Roberto said.

"I wonder if Tisdel's ever coming back," I said.

"Maybe he went to Canada!"

Richard came over and looked at me. "Now *that* was nice."

The next day, the great Robert Tisdel showed up with his father, who demanded to speak with Brother Raymond with his son present. The three of them went into the hall together. A low rumble of "wows" and "mans" filled the classroom. Minutes later, Tisdel came back inside and sat down, a smirk on his face. Brother Raymond entered shortly thereafter, subdued and red faced.

The suspense was unbearable. When lunchtime came, we surrounded Tisdel like he was a rock star signing autographs.

"I don't really want to talk about it," he said.

"No way, man!" I said. "At least give us the headline version."

"My father threatened to take Brother Raymond to court."

"What?"

"And that if he hit me again, he would have to fight him."

Man!

The Tisdel incident changed everything. I found myself walking with an extra spring in my step, as if it was me who had defied Brother Raymond, me who had saved the world in one breathtaking act of defiance. So I guess that, in the smallest of ways, the excitement of 1968 was not entirely lost on me.

Brother Raymond changed, too, as if he had slapped himself in the face and said, "Thanks, I needed that." Slowly but surely, in ways more understated than pronounced, our teacher and school principal became more good-humored, relaxed and approachable. Like we were no longer the enemy. "Maybe you should just study harder," he took to saying when a simple math solution was forgotten. Or he would smile in resignation when someone in class just couldn't get beyond a D in tests.

Yeah, Tisdel changed everything. Appropriately enough, the guy would play a role in another epic moment, except that this one involved me too—and I was to lead it.

TWELVE

The Greatest Race Ever

The runner from St. Thomas Aquinas took off his maroon and gold sweatpants, revealing ebony legs that seemed to begin at his rib cage. Each leg was dotted with spools of dark hair, far too many to belong to someone from junior high school.

"What is this dude? Twenty fucking years old?" Roberto asked, looking at the guy and then at me.

"Maybe he got left back," I shrugged, mesmerized by the runner's strong legs, which perfectly matched his muscled torso. His tank top and shorts were the same bright colors as his sweats and appeared to be made of satin. I looked down at his track shoes, a glistening gold pair of soft leather running cleats.

"Man, those are some nice cleats."

"Probably stole 'em," said Roberto.

I laughed and squinted into the cloudless June sky. It was a Saturday morning, and we were sitting in the middle of the track field at Mount St. Michael's Academy for a daylong track and field meet featuring runners from Catholic elementary and middle schools. Mount St. Michael's was a Catholic high school nestled on twenty-plus pastoral acres on Murdock Avenue in the northernmost Bronx.

Roberto, Tisdel, a classmate named Ruben and I were representing St. Luke's as members of its 880-yard relay team. Unlike our brethren at St. Thomas Aquinas, we sported no uniforms of any kind. Each of us had on different-color running shorts, all of cheap polyester. We did, however, wear matching red T-shirts, which at least identified us a team.

I had joined the track team in the seventh grade, at the urging of Brother Lawrence, who in between teaching and bouts of madness was St. Luke's athletic director. In addition to running gym class and overseeing afterschool basketball, Brother Lawrence also coached the track team. Well, perhaps *coach* is a generous word. Brother Lawrence sported a clipboard, a stubbed No. 2 pencil and a whistle. He was a guy dressed like a coach.

Coach Lawrence had discovered I was fast in one of the many practices held in Randall's Island, a 400-acre park anchoring Manhattan, Queens and the Bronx and bordered by the East River and the Harlem River. We got to Randall's via a pedestrian walkway alongside the Triborough Bridge, accessed from a ramp on 132nd Street and Cypress Avenue across from the 7UP factory.

Randall's was ideal for racing, with numerous tree-lined paths wide enough for a half-a-dozen runners. We used the lampposts as distance markers and occasionally the discus thrower statue about 100 yards away. Brother Lawrence would line us up and blow his whistle, and off we would zoom.

I won every sprint race that I ran—usually a distance of 60 or 100 yards. It was a thrilling experience, and I soon discovered what it meant to be in a zone, feeling a weightlessness where all that was visual was the finish line, the audio a blend of exhales and pounding sneakers.

What made it better was that, unlike my defensiveness about being a top student, here was a pride that I could wear openly. No teasing, no put-downs, only praise and quite bit of envy. I was fast. No—the *fastest*.

And it felt great.

Soon, I was competing in indoor and outdoor meets organized by the Police Athletic League or some Catholic school association. I won at least one medal in every track meet I took part in—mostly gold or silver. The medals, with the head of the Greek god Mercury wearing a winged helmet engraved on them, came in a plastic case. My specialty became the 220-yard dash.

I'd run many terrific races, but none as exciting and scary as the one about to take place at Mount St. Michael's.

◆ ◆ ◆

I nearly fell over when I overheard Daddy Long Legs, as Roberto christened him, telling a girl that, yes, he was running in the 880 relay and that, yes, his team would definitely win.

"It's guaranteed," he told her in a baritone voice. She cooed.

"Yo, that dude's running in *our* race, man," I said.

"We should get his birth certificate," Roberto said. "You think we can take them, Dave?"

I didn't answer as I pondered our chances. Roberto and I were both fast and had relay experience. Tisdel was fast, too, but had never run a relay before. Ruben, on the other hand, was a chain smoker who had good speed but who practically passed out after every practice. He was here only because Kevin Quealy, the other fast runner from our school, had come down with the flu.

My worries mounted when the rest of the St. Thomas's 4 x 220 relay team joined Daddy Long Legs. They looked just like he did: too old to be in junior high and too fast to be challenged. When they began bouncing up and down on the balls of their feet in unison, their body language screamed, "We will *dust* your asses."

I realized what was happening: I was being psyched out, beaten before the race had even begun. That had never happened before.

I began *willing* myself to feel positive. "C'mon," I told my teammates, clapping my hands. "We're from killer's land; we can beat these guys. Where's Brother Lawrence?"

"At the gate, smoking a cigarette," Ruben replied. "What I should be doing, since we ain't gonna win shit anyway."

"Damn! I forgot my track shoes," Tisdel said suddenly.

"Are you kidding me?" I said. "The race is about to freaking start, bro'!"

"I'll fix things. Watch," he said.

Tisdel jogged over to the bleachers and got into an animated conversation with a group of guys from St. Jerome's, another school in the Mott Haven neighborhood. To my surprise, Tisdel came back with a pair of light blue running cleats.

"How the hell did you do that?" Roberto asked. "Did you know those dudes?"

"Nah, but one guy said it was cool to borrow his tracks. He's in the long jump, but he ain't jumping till this afternoon. You just gotta know how to talk to people."

"They look big," I said. "What size are they?"

"Ten. I'm an eight, but it's cool."

I sighed out loud and made the sign of the cross.

The three other teams competing in the 880-yard relay came out of the locker room and onto the field. All of them wore color-matching running outfits.

The Greatest Race Ever

Ruben came up to me, coughing. "Yo, Dave, let's at least place second. Pretty uniforms don't mean a thing, right?"

I wasn't listening. Brother Lawrence approached us smelling like an ashtray and wished us good luck. I guess. I wasn't listening to him either. I was trying to regain my confidence, to shake off the feelings of intimidation.

"Attention, please," the loudspeaker blared. "Boys' 880 relay, please report to the starting area." It was time.

The order was me first, Roberto second and Ruben third. Tisdel had the anchor leg.

"Make believe the cops are chasing you," Roberto told Tisdel.

"No problem," Tisdel answered as he shuffled onto the track in his oversized cleats.

As luck would have it, Daddy Long Legs was starting for St. Thomas, and he was right next to me. There was no breeze, and the sun was hot.

The official with the starter pistol nodded toward the starting line. "Runners, on your mark."

I got into starting position, our school's lone, dented silver baton held softly in my right hand between thumb and index finger.

Lord, please give me the race of my life.

"Get set."

I hunched in the set position, sweat building on my tense body.

Bang! I was off before the sound of the shot even finished. I'd never had such a good start, and I felt like I was literally flying. My arms were pumping, my chest was out, and my canvas running sneakers (newly purchased from Sam's Sporting Goods) were burning asphalt. I was in my familiar zone, and the rest of the world collapsed into just my speed and me. After about 50 yards, I glanced quickly to my right; the guy from St. Thomas wasn't there. Since no one was in front of me, it could only mean that I was in the lead.

That realization, not even a second long, gave my adrenaline such a lift that I felt instantly unbeatable. I accelerated. By the time I reached Roberto, my lead, I was told later, was close to 10 yards, a large distance in a short sprint race. The baton passing went perfectly. I then noticed that Daddy Long Legs had been in *last* place.

Roberto was in his own zone, and by the time he passed the baton to Ruben, our lead over the second-place team, St. Agnes, had increased to about 20 yards, an almost insurmountable amount to make up. Or so I thought until Ruben reached the halfway mark of his relay leg, where he seemed to run out of gas, his young smoker's lungs failing him.

When Tisdel got the baton, our lead had been cut in half. But my anxiety was short-lived. Maybe it was the big shoes or the imagined fleeing from the law, but Tisdel cooked. He actually increased our margin of victory by the time he blew past the finish line. We had won; the St. Thomas Aquinas team finished third.

Roberto, Ruben and I ran to Tisdel, whooping and shouting. Brother Lawrence came dashing toward us with a smile as big as the track field.

"God has blessed St. Luke's this morning!" he exclaimed.

A track official from the archdiocese came up and told him that in addition to our individual medals, the school was going to receive a trophy. Our not-really-a-coach looked like he was going to cry. It was, as far as I knew, the first track trophy St. Luke's had ever won.

Then Brother Lawrence did a most remarkable thing. He hugged each one of us tightly, beaming as if all the demons had finally been lifted from his dandruff-filled shoulders.

THIRTEEN

"Way to Go!"

On June 23, 1969, I graduated from St. Luke's. The Young Lords Party, a Puerto Rican activist group, was organizing in the area, and the Fifth Dimension was singing about the dawning of the Age of Aquarius. Shag haircuts made their debut, and salsa music had become an international phenomenon.

I would feel the impact of all these things.

Our graduation caps and gowns were a marine blue, shimmering like the waters of Luquillo Beach in Puerto Rico. Underneath I wore a dark blue suit, white shirt and, saints be praised, a pair of classy dress shoes.

The emotional highlight of the ceremony was my classmate, Gary Bailey, being carried into the church on his father's arms. Gary had been a victim of a serious hit-and-run on the street in front of the schoolyard, which was closed to traffic during lunch and recess. In April, a Cadillac had pulled out quickly and run Gary over. For a while it was unclear whether he was going to survive.

Julio had witnessed the accident and described it in gory detail to our class. Death and near-death are fascinating at any age, and all I could picture was Gary being squished like a Raggedy Ann doll, the Cadillac's tires thumping over his exposed bones. For days it was hard to think of anything else.

A standing ovation greeted Gary when he was carried inside St. Luke's Church on graduation day. He was wearing his cap and gown, and there wasn't a dry eye in the place. And then came the announcement: "And the Medal of Excellence for Overall Academic Achievement goes to... David Pérez!"

My final report card read zero for absence and zero for lateness. My lowest grade was 94.

For that one brief but illustrious moment, I shed my defensiveness about my smarts, strutted up to the altar and shook Father Ryan's hand. He winked at me, the Baby Jesus fiasco of Christmas Mass forgotten, or at least forgiven. Father Ryan pinned the gold medal on my gown, and I floated back to my pew. Chino applauded for me, and Mami wiped away a happy tear.

For our yearbook we received four-by-six-inch spiral-bound leather notebooks with the words *Archdiocese of New York* imprinted in Gothic lettering. The diploma inside certified that I, "David M. Pérez," was of "Good Christian Character and had satisfactorily completed the course of study prescribed by the Archdiocese and the New York State Education Department."

The front page of the yearbook displayed a photo of St. Luke's Church, gray bricked, with two Volkswagen Beetles parked in front. The Rev. Gerald J. Ryan was pictured underneath, as was our teacher and principal, Brother Raymond Shirvell. It was the first time I had seen his full name.

Graduation photos of the class of '69 (boys and girls got separate yearbooks) filled the inside pages: more than thirty smiling faces, and a few sour ones.

Outside was the usual postgraduation circus: graduates shouting, "We made it" and "Thank God I'm done." Friends and family exclaiming that their loved ones looked beautiful and "so grown up!"

My mother wore a light orange dress and matching hat adorned with a fishnet veil. In between snapping Polaroids, she accepted congratulations from assorted teachers and parents.

"You must be proud of your smart son," a lady said to her.

"He's a track star, too," Mami said.

Pops wasn't there, but I was used to his absence by now. I knew he would have an envelope of money for me at home, however. I hoped he had hit the numbers again.

George, all six feet of him, embraced me. "Way to go, little brother!"

While George and I had the usual sibling rivalries, we unfailingly rooted for each other. In September, I would be joining him as a student at Cardinal Hayes High School, a top-notch school located not too far from Yankee Stadium.

"You going to join the track team there, Dave?"

"Yeah, maybe try out for the freshman football team, too."

"I'll stick to drawing."

George had matured into quite the artist, drawing humorous caricatures of his classmates and realistic-looking superheroes. He'd even invented his own characters, like the Kleptomaniac Kid, who could look at an object and make it appear in his hand.

All of my close friends were heading for a public high school: Roberto and Julio were going to DeWitt Clinton, a tough school where the "bad" kids went—bad because their grades stank and bad because they were hip. Often the two went together. Chino was off to Dodge Vocational, a school for boys *and* girls.

At home, Pops had left a couple of twenty-dollar bills on my bed for me. I was disappointed he wasn't home; his "hanging with his friends," as Mami put it with a sigh, was becoming the norm in our house. I held out the hope that Pops wouldn't come home late. Maybe he'd offer to take me to another Yankee game.

I changed into my sharkskins and Cons and joined my buddies for a much-deserved celebration. Roberto, Julio and I stopped by a bodega on St. Ann's Avenue and bought a quart of Colt 45. The owner of the store, unsurprisingly, didn't ask us for ID. I'd seen ten-year-olds purchase beer and cigarettes—even Bambú rolling papers.

At the Big Park we talked about one day trying marijuana, which we would cop from the pet shop on 138th Street. The store dealt pot from the back door.

"I hear it's laced with embalming fluid," Julio said.

"The herb?" I asked.

"It's true," Roberto said. "That's so it can fuck you up even better."

That was the new happening thing. You couldn't just get high. You needed to get "fucked up."

Roberto unscrewed the bottle cap and poured beer on the ground, "to honor the dead." I wondered where the ritual came from, but didn't ask. Which dead was he referring to?

Roberto sipped long and hard. "Ah, nice and cold," he said, licking his lips.

He passed me the bottle, and I wiped the top. I repeated the honoring the dead ritual, but only with a drop. No sense wasting good malt liquor.

The cold beer rattled my teeth and tasted great. It wasn't the first time I'd drunk beer; one Christmas I had sampled a Ballantine in my kitchen when no one was looking. It tasted flat, causing me to wonder what Pops found in it. The Colt 45 had a much richer flavor, foamy and easy on the tongue.

"So Dave with the Medal of Excellence!" Roberto said. "And going to Cardinal Hayes. Strict there, I hear."

"Yeah, they even got a dean of discipline. Guy used to be a sheriff or something like that. Hey, but after St. Luke's how hard can it be, right?"

"Where's Chino?" Julio asked.

Roberto said Chino had gone to St. Mary's immediately following graduation, to hang with the boxers there.

"Chino's getting tight with them." Roberto said.

"Good for him," I said and handed the Colt 45 to Julio, who almost polished off the bottle with a huge gulp. Julio wore new, big-framed glasses, with thick lenses that magnified his beady eyes, earning him the nickname Focus, a moniker that would stay with him forever.

"I'm through with Catholic school," Julio said. "I wanna take it easy for once, you know. I'm gonna miss St. Luke's in a way, though. Some crazy times."

"Crazy," Roberto said

"Crazy," I repeated.

As we finished the quart, Julio fished out a Kool cigarette from his front shirt pocket. He'd bought the "loose" for a nickel from the bodega. Julio fired up, took a deep drag and passed the cigarette to Roberto, who also inhaled deeply.

Roberto passed me the cigarette, and I inhaled. The menthol seared my lungs, and I stifled a cough.

"Your first cig?" Roberto asked.

"Nah, man," I lied. "Just my first Kool."

Julio said I was full of shit. I said I was, and we all laughed.

Author's Note

This book was my sincere effort to record my childhood experiences. Memory is slippery, selective and often unattainable. At times I had conflicting versions of events from friends and family. So like all memoirists, I had to pick and chose. I downplayed some "facts" and highlighted others, despite my storyteller's tendency to embellish a tale (ask my kids!) In the end, I reminded myself that memoir is not only about facts. More importantly, it's about truth.

Note: I did change some names so as not to startle old friends. I purposely left out most last names. A couple of characters are composites.

Thanks

any people made *Wow!* possible, and I thank each and every one of you.

A special *abrazo* to Monique Parker, my fellow writer, editor, and collaborator who saw this manuscript through innumerable phases. I'll always treasure your keen eye and unwavering encouragement and friendship.

Thank you, Summer Wood, for providing me with valuable manuscript evaluation and expert advice on all aspects of writing and publishing. *Gracias tambien* to Michael Thompson and my son Jase Miles-Pérez for the fabulous feedback on my first draft. Your insights improved the book in ways I could never do on my own. Thank you to my daughter Belinda Maria Pérez for your wonderful comments (and for scanning those images for me!).

To my brother, George Pérez, aka Papo: Here's to our first collaboration, a wow! experience in itself!

Thank you 11B Press and the fabulous Dean Throntveit and Jelayne Miles for making all this happen, and for providing the vision for this exciting company. Thank you, Diana Rico, for your copyediting skills and support. Thank you, Barbara Scott, for your "final eyes" on copyediting and proofreading. Thank you, Andrea Watson, for your expert proofreading and for coming through in a pinch. Thank you, Barry Kerrigan and the entire Desktop Miracles team for the top-notch book designing work.

Thanks go to Diana Kash, Ellen Schecter, Dan Rous, Maura Mulligan and Hilda Meltzer (RIP), my New York City writing group who helped develop this book in its infancy. Others to thank include Patricia Kenet, Magdalene Smith, Millie Ehrlich, Helen Rynaski, Jeff Haas. Thank you, Lenny Foster, for the great author's photo. Thank you, Moby Dickens Bookshop in Taos, New Mexico.

Thank you Kimmel Harding Nelson Center for the Arts for the six-week residency in Nebraska City where much of this book was crafted. Thank you Society of the Muse of the Southwest for allowing me to read at your Writer's Series. Thank you Robin Collier and Cultural Energy for the audio recordings.

A special shout out goes to Danny and his family for being my constant connection to growing up in the South Bronx.

And to my precious wife, Veronica: Thank you for being my biggest fan.

About the Author

David Pérez grew up in the South Bronx, part of the first generation of Puerto Ricans born and raised in New York City. His first foray into writing was at fifteen, when he penned the short story "As the City Sleeps," which featured him and his buddies as a neighborhood gang called the Dirty Dozen taking on the Mafia and getting themselves killed. His brother George illustrated the cover, a precursor to the artwork he's done for *Wow!*

By the early 1980s, Pérez was a reporter and managing editor for *Workers World* newspaper, a socialist weekly. He wrote hundreds of articles and pamphlets, including *The Class Roots of Racism* and *Capitalism, Genetics and the Natural Order*. In the mid-1990s, Pérez's personal essay about fatherhood, "When Dolls Talk," was published in *El Andar*.

In Taos, New Mexico, Pérez joined the staff of *Tempo*, the weekly arts and entertainment magazine of *The Taos News*, where he wrote dozens of features on the local arts scene, as well as investigative articles on bottled water and the dangers of cell phones. He's also a regular contributor to *New Mexico Magazine*.

Currently, Pérez earns his living as a freelance editor and writer, and is involved in community theater. The father of two adult children, he divides his time between New York City and Taos with his wife, poet Veronica Golos.

Pérez is available for readings, performances and interviews. He can be reached at david@11bpress.com, or you can visit his website: www.davidperezwow.com.

About the Artist

George Pérez is an internationally acclaimed, award-winning comic book artist and writer, known for his epic storytelling and hyper-detailed artwork on such titles as *JLA/Avengers, The New Teen Titans, Crisis on Infinite Earths,* and *Wonder Woman,* among scores of others. You can follow him on Facebook and on his official fan site, www.george-perez.com.

About 11B Press

11B Press is a division of 11B Productions LLC, an umbrella that also includes 11B Pictures. The mission of both the film and publishing ventures is to create exciting and groundbreaking projects that both inspire and entertain. 11B will feature established and emerging artists. For more information, please visit www.11bproductions.com.

www.ingramcontent.com/pod-product-compliance
Lightning Source LLC
Chambersburg PA
CBHW060809050426
42449CB00008B/1610